What They're Saying About *Keep F*!#ing Going*

"The KFG Formula shares a proven framework to navigate challenges and change, all while meeting you exactly where you are in your own personal journey."

—**Russell Wilson**, NFL quarterback (Denver Broncos, Seattle Seahawks, Pittsburgh Steelers), nine-time Pro Bowl quarterback, 2021 Walter Payton NFL Man of the Year; cofounder, Limitless Minds

"If you are looking for a powerful formula for living your life, the KFG Formula is for you!"

—**Jack Canfield**, coauthor of the *Chicken Soup for the Soul®* series and *The Success Principles™: How to Get from Where You Are to Where You Want to Be*

"I decided to attend a first responder mental health conference—for me. I needed to learn how to better care for myself. On November 3, 2023, you and I crossed paths. You told your story of how you were at the Route 91 Festival. When the chaos erupted, you could tell who was there to help, and you remembered people helping others get to safety.

As I heard your story, I couldn't help but think that my friend, Charleston—an off-duty first responder—that his last act that night was to help you, and others like you get safely out. This helped me find closure in his death. I truly appreciate you sharing your story. It will certainly help others in life. I will never forget how I felt when you said to *Keep . . . F*!#ing . . . Going*."

—**Former Las Vegas police officer** impacted by the events of Oct. 1, 2017 (wishes to remain anonymous)

THE KFG FORMULA

A Step-By-Step Guide to
Successfully Navigate Change

KRISTA RYAN

Clovercroft Publishing
Franklin, TN

A Step-By-Step Guide to Successfully Navigate Change

KFG®

Published by Clovercroft Publishing, Franklin, Tennessee
CloverCroftPublishingGroup.com

Edited by Robert Irvin

Interior Design and Cover Design by Suzanne Lawing

Printed in the United States of America

ISBN: 978-1-956370-31-7 (print)

DEDICATION

Chris, Mason, Brooklynn, and Grace.
I love you more than all the king crab legs in the world.

To you. I see you. Keep going.

This poem by Heartsill Wilson was displayed for years in my Grandmother Tutu's office. When she passed away in 2016 it was gifted to me and is now displayed on my vision board in my office as a daily reminder.

This is the beginning of a new day. God has given me this day to use as I will. I can waste it or use it for good. What I do today is important, because I'm exchanging a day of my life for it. When tomorrow comes, this day will be gone forever, leaving in its place something I have traded for it. I want it to be gain, not loss; good, not evil; success, not failure; in order that I shall not regret the price I paid for it.

CONTENTS

KFG: How the Concept Came to Be 9

Step One: Know 29

Step Two: Focus 67

Step Three: Go 89

KFG: The Conclusion (For Now) 127

Share Your KFG Story 135

Reflection and Action—Teams and Organization 137

Reflection and Action—Individuals and Book Clubs 139

Resources to Support Your Success 141

Acknowledgments 145

About the Author and Speaker 149

KFG: HOW THE CONCEPT CAME TO BE

Keep fucking going . . .

That was the only thought going through my mind as I ran for my life through the streets of Las Vegas. I was trying to escape the shooter who had opened fire that night on the Harvest Music Festival.

It was October 1, 2017.

The day my life changed forever.

Keep fucking going . . .

* * * * *

Hours earlier, my husband, Chris, and I and two other couples—friends of ours who, along with us, wanted to celebrate the kids being back in school, something we would do with an adult getaway—had been lounging by the pool at the MGM Grand in Las Vegas. We had planned this vacation around the Route 91 Harvest Music Festival, the second time Chris and I attended this festival. The last two days and nights had been spent relaxing by the pool throughout the day, then getting ready and going to the concerts in the evening. We'd enjoyed doing a whole lot of nothing but celebrating ourselves, having fun together, laughing so hard our stomachs hurt, and listening to great music. It was pure bliss.

That night, as the sun set, we walked across the street from the hotel to the venue, excited to see the headliner, Jason Aldean. The venue held twenty-two thousand people, most of whom stood around in groups or sat in lawn chairs placed side by side. The diehard fans who were willing to brave the Nevada heat during the day had first dibs on the spots closest to the stage. Crowds of people swarmed in at the last minute before the night's headliners began, and this created a bottleneck of concertgoers that was trying to get through security and into the venue.

We were among that crowd. All of us were on the same mission: to claim our piece of land to watch our favorite artists under the Las Vegas stars. In just a few minutes, though, my husband and I got separated. Just before the music started, he told me he was going to find the largest belt buckle he could before the music started. Then he was off, and I lost him among the throngs of people, including vendors selling food and merchandise. There was barely controlled chaos everywhere.

As the sun set that night, musicians Big & Rich took the stage and performed a sing-along of "God Bless America." My arms prickled with goose bumps and I shed a few tears as we all sang together in harmony. It felt as if we were all united in that moment, thousands of us holding our cellphones in the air, singing as one. The beauty of the moment was surreal.

That would turn out to be the last moment of peace we'd have that night.

Jason Aldean hit the stage, and I thought, *I have to find Chris. Enough with the belt buckle already—we're here for the music!*

After a bit of time, and multiple text exchanges, I found him, but I was frustrated that he had wandered off in search of that belt buckle. "I didn't know where you were!" I said, quite loudly.

He didn't understand my frustration, but I was stubborn—and still irritated. Chris, hungry and annoyed with my response, said he was going to grab a bite to eat from a vendor. I decided not to go with him, so he walked off again. I hoisted myself onto a table at a stand that was not being used and waited.

As I looked around, it started to dawn on me that I was alone. I was separated from everyone I knew, all due to my own stubbornness, among a crowd of twenty-two thousand, in the dark.

I pulled out my phone to call Chris and saw that my battery was at 2 percent. *Oh shit, this isn't good.* Chris was always telling me to charge my phone because I was very good at letting the battery run low. Tonight was one of those nights.

I texted one of my friends: "My phone's about to die. I have no idea where you guys are."

Just before the screen faded to black, I saw that it was ten o'clock.

Three minutes later, the first gunshots started.

RUNNING FOR OUR LIVES

Something is very wrong. I could feel it in my gut.

I was toward the back of the venue, so I couldn't clearly see what was going on near the stage. People near me were looking around in all directions, trying to figure out *what* we were hearing. Someone said, "Oh, it's fireworks near the main stage." But we didn't see any bright sparkles lighting up the night sky.

A few seconds later, I heard screaming. The crowd descended into chaos. The *pop-pop-pop* sound did not stop. It seemed to get even louder, and then it became clear exactly what it was: *gunfire.*

I'm from Minnesota, so I've been around guns and hunting most of my life. This wasn't a hunting rifle, and it didn't sound like a handgun either. I'd never heard a machine gun in person—only on TV and in movies—but that's exactly what it sounded like.

The screaming continued, louder and louder as more and more people joined in. Some people started running toward us, away from the stage. A woman ran by with blood covering her yellow tank top. She was silent, her eyes filled with terror. My heart felt as if it dropped out of my chest. *What the hell is going on? This can't really be happening.*

I jumped off the table I'd been sitting on and fell to the ground. I could still hear the *pop-pop-pop* exploding through the air. People dove for cover on the hard pavement, all of us covering our heads and piling on top of each other, trying to get as low as possible and protect each other from what we now understood as gunshots. But it didn't matter which way we ran or where we tried to hide. We couldn't escape the shots raining down all around us.

Bullets ricocheted off the pavement and slammed into bodies. We had no idea where they were coming from. I thought two or more people must have been shooting at each other on the ground, near where we were. It never crossed my mind that it could be someone in a window on the thirty-second floor firing down at us, as we would later learn.

A startling realization quickly hit us: we couldn't continue to cower in place; we were all sitting ducks in the open. There was a pause in the gunshots. A man yelled, "Go now! Go, go, *go*!"

Everything was in black and white. I was running as fast as I could, but it seemed like I was moving in slow motion. Now I heard the gunshots start again.

All of the people piled around me scrambled off the ground, and we started running for our lives. Everything was in black and white. I was running as fast as I could, but it seemed like I was moving in slow motion. Now I heard the gunshots start again. I didn't make any conscious choice where to go; my body just *moved*.

I felt guilt tangle with the fear in my stomach as I ran. I saw people around me who were hurt, and I was stepping on them, barely slowing as I did. My flip-flops had come off at some point, and I felt the flesh of someone's leg under my feet. I splashed through blood—and kept going.

Once I was running, I remember thinking, *That's it. . . . I am not stopping or taking cover again. I am getting out.*

And that's when the thought that would become my mantra that night—and into my future—flashed through my brain: just keep fucking going.

Hundreds and hundreds of people were on the ground, injured or trying to stay down, out of the line of fire. Those of us who were up and running were scrambling to find a way out of the venue—but we were caged. The fences designed to keep people out were now trapping us in with the bullets still raining around us.

I reached out and grabbed the hand of the woman running next to me. She looked like she was in her late fifties, and she was screaming hysterically in Spanish. I dragged her over to the chain-link fence at the edge of the concert grounds. Hundreds of people were pulling on it as hard as we could, trying to break it down, but it didn't budge.

We'd have to scale it.

I looked down at my bare feet and thought, *Damn, I wish I had cowboy boots!* Those who had boots were able to get their footing on the links of the fence much faster than those of us who were barefoot or wearing sandals.

I heard it again: *Keep. Fucking. Going.* Each word punctuated by the never-ceasing gunfire.

I convinced the woman whose hand I'd grabbed to climb the fence. "Come on. You can do it. You can do it! You gotta get over!"

She was really struggling. I didn't know how the hell she was going to get over that fence. But there were people waiting behind us to climb that fence, and every one of their lives were in danger. I hoisted her up and over, throwing her the last couple of feet to the ground. I knew she might be injured, and I worried that she'd break a leg and not be able to continue running, but I had no choice. We all had to get out of there.

She landed with a hard *thud* on the other side, and fortunately she got right up. I scrambled over the fence as fast as I could, grabbed her hand again, and we started running into the pitch-black night.

I looked back once as we ran and saw other people fall off the fence and hit the ground. I didn't know if they were jumping or if they'd been shot.

It was just chaos.

Keep . . . fucking . . . going.

After that, I didn't look back. I yelled to the woman I was running with, "Whatever happens, don't stop running! Even if I let go of your hand, you have to keep going as fast as you can. Don't turn around, and *don't stop!*"

I don't know if she understood me, but I didn't let go, and we didn't stop. I'm not a fast runner, but I was dragging her along with me, farther and farther from the venue, from the gunshots, from the blood on the ground and on people who were injured or worse. I didn't know where we were going—just *away.*

I don't know if she understood me, but I didn't let go, and we didn't stop. I'm not a fast runner, but I was dragging her along with me.

The farther we got from the venue, the quieter it got, just the sound of our ragged breathing and the footfalls of other people fleeing around us. Some of them were trying to get people in nearby houses and apartments to let them in, but nobody opened their doors. They must have been scared out of their minds seeing hundreds of people running through the streets, some of them bloody, and hearing them pound on the doors, screaming, "Please, let us in!"

I don't blame them for not opening the doors and letting people in. It was pure, unbelievable chaos. Everyone was scared, and no one knew where to find safety.

So we kept running.

GOING BACK

Eventually, we got really far away and felt like we could stop at a gas station to catch our breath. The woman I was with called her daughter, who lived in Las Vegas, and her daughter drove to the station to pick her up.

I helped the woman into the passenger seat, and her daughter turned to me and said, "Please, come with us. I'll take you to my house. You'll be safe, and you can stay there as long as you need."

"I can't," I told her. "My husband and friends are back there. I'm not leaving them—I have to go back!"

It was not an option for me to take cover at her house, even though I was scared out of my mind. I didn't know where Chris was, if he was safe, if he had gotten out. I didn't have any way of getting ahold of him or our friends, so I was going back. They had to be there somewhere.

She looked at me like I was crazy—and it was an insane decision. I knew this wasn't making any sense, but leaving Chris and the others behind wasn't an option. The woman and her daughter drove away.

Keep fucking going.

I had no idea what I was going back to. I just knew that I was once again running through the dark—this time running *toward* the danger—and now I was alone again.

As I ran back toward the venue, I could feel emotion and shock taking over my body. I started to shake uncontrollably. Then my whole body just gave out, my knees buckling, and I hit the sidewalk. As I tried to push myself up, I felt someone strong grab me by the shoulders and lift me off the ground. A tall man wearing a big cowboy hat was

I could feel emotion and shock taking over my body. I started to shake uncontrollably. Then my whole body just gave out, my knees buckling.

holding me up so my eyes met his. With a strong and stern voice, he asked, "Are you hurt?"

"No," I told him. My voice was shaky, and I barely could get the words out. "My legs just gave out."

"Then you have to get up. You have to keep running," he said with calmness, yet also with plenty of authority in his voice. "You can't stop here out in the wide open; you're in danger. You have to *keep going.*"

His words echoed the ones that had been going through my head ever since I started running: *keep fucking going.* They were my spark of light in the midst of the nightmare dark, and they gave me the kick in the butt I needed to get clarity on my next steps: I was alone in the middle of downtown Las Vegas. It wasn't safe there, it wasn't safe back at the venue, it didn't feel safe anywhere. All I knew was that I had to get back to Chris and my friends, so I took a deep breath and started running again . . .

As I got close to the venue, a group of people huddled behind a sign advertising the Las Vegas nightlife yelled for me to stop. I didn't—I had to keep going, had to find Chris and our friends—so they grabbed me and pulled me into their hiding place. One woman put on her stern mom voice and said, "You are not going back in there; it's not safe. I don't care that you want to look for your husband and friends. We are not letting you do that. You're staying here with us until we figure out what to do."

They were complete strangers who saw I was alone and putting myself in harm's way, and they weren't about to allow it because I clearly wasn't making sense. Still, no one knew if the shooter had been apprehended, or how many shooters there were, or even where the shots were coming from.

There were so many people swarming everywhere—concertgoers, first responders, police, military units, the FBI. People had guns out. Other people were limping past, injured either from being shot or from the mad crush to get out. It was like being in a war zone, one that none of us had signed up for.

The guardian angels who held me behind that sign took the decision about returning to the venue out of my hands. They kept me safe, and eventually they helped me reconnect with Chris. The woman who had spoken up—whose name I would learn was Heather—pulled out her phone. I gave her Chris's number, and she called him to let him know I was with her.

But he didn't answer! Terrifying thoughts whirled through my mind: *His phone's dead, and I won't be able to find him. . . .* Or, *Maybe he lost his phone. . . .* Or, *Oh my God, what if he's hurt??*

As it turns out, Chris had seen an unknown number come up on his caller ID, and because he was in his own crazy world of trying to figure out what was going on, he didn't answer. A few minutes later, however, he realized it was a Las Vegas number, and he called back. Heather told him that I was with her, that I was safe. He said, "Okay, thank you," and hung up—but immediately had an uneasy feeling. He hadn't actually heard my voice, and no one knew who they could trust in all of this. He called back and said, "Put Krista on the phone. I need to hear her voice. I'm not going anywhere until I hear from her that she's safe, that she's with you."

I got on the phone and said, "Chris, it's me. I'm here, I'm safe. Where are you!?"

He had found two of our friends, and the three of them stuck together, eventually making their way out of the venue and to a gas station where a triage area had been set up and where they had hunkered down. The other couple had fled out a different exit. They were safe, together.

Heather said she would pin-drop our location on his phone so Chris could find us. We were so far apart—I had run what felt like miles from the venue before turning back.

As I saw Chris and our friends walking toward us, I ran across the street to meet them. I should have felt relieved to be reunited with Chris, but I was still so scared. You may think it was like in the movies—running across the street and embracing your loved ones in pure bliss and emotion—but it was not like that at all. In real life, everything is so different. I was still scared. In shock. My body tired. All was chaos. People were yelling at me—I don't know if they were security or police—because they didn't know who was safe.

Even after I reached Chris and our friends, we felt vulnerable being on the street, so we scrambled to hide, to find shelter and safety, to stay out of the way.

You may think it was like in the movies—running across the street and embracing your loved ones in pure bliss and emotion—but it was not like that at all.

RETURNING HOME

When we finally made it back to the hotel, it was like walking into a scene from a nightmare. In the casino, some people were silent, in shock. Others were screaming or crying, the terror still so flooding their bodies that they couldn't believe they were safe. Still others were playing slot machines and going about their normal lives, when just on the other side of the wall hundreds of people had been shot.

It was an absolutely bizarre reality.

We went into the bathroom to clean up and wash the blood off our bodies—most of which wasn't ours. There were other people in the restroom doing the same. We were all just scrubbing away, trying to get other people's blood off our faces, arms, and legs.

When we entered the lobby of our hotel, we were greeted by an eerie silence. It was completely empty. We learned later that the hotel staff was on lockdown; they were all in hiding. They didn't even know what had happened, just that it was bad, and that they were told to lock down.

We finally made it back to our room. It felt like a lifetime, but unbelievably it had only been an hour or so since the shooting had started.

Chris and I just . . . sat there. It was quiet. We didn't know how to process what had happened. We didn't know what to think. The news stations hadn't broken the story yet, but as accounts of what happened were posted to social media—and as the news eventually hit the airwaves—our phones started to blow up with phone calls and messages from family and friends asking if we were okay.

That's when it started to feel real. *Were* we okay? *What* had we just been through?

I was in shock that whole night and into the next morning. I didn't know who to call or what to say. My first phone call was to my brother. As we were talking, I looked down and realized I was still wearing the same dirty, blood-stained clothes from the night before.

"I have to go," I told him. "I have to change."

Then I looked over at Chris and saw that he had on two different sandals—he had lost one of his and picked up someone else's that had fallen off. His feet were covered in dried blood, so I sat on the shower floor and scrubbed them as hard as I could. I wanted all that blood off him, to remove all traces of what had happened. But how could we scrub away all the evidence of this horrific event and just go back to our normal lives? It seemed impossible, but I told myself yet again: *just keep fucking going . . .*

I wanted all that blood off him, to remove all traces of what had happened.

* * * * *

Later that morning, the six of us sat outside the hotel with our luggage, waiting for our ride to the airport, and we didn't look at each other. We didn't talk. We hadn't shared stories about what had happened to each of us the night before. We just sat in silence, still in shock, baffled by these events that didn't even make sense, trying to forget their horrors.

If anything was going to remind us that we couldn't just walk away from what had happened, it was that flight back home. It was full of people from the concert getting the hell out of Vegas. People just like us. Stunned. Emotional. Shell-shocked. Horrified. Everyone was on edge, and many people were crying. A disagreement broke out at the travel counter among anxious passengers wanting to get home. The tension was high; anxiety was felt by everyone. I was seated on the plane next to a woman who was traveling back to her home to deal with a death in her family. She silently cried the entire flight. I sat numb—I was unable to communicate or show empathy. The rest of the passengers were silent. I don't remember any conversations. There was no communication about what had tragically happened. There were no stories shared.

No one knew what to say or do, including me. It was eerie. It was scary. It was lonely. It was sad.

There was terrible air turbulence on that flight, the worst I'd ever experienced. I thought, *I made it through last night, and now I'm going to die on this plane.* Irrational? Heck yes! But my body and emotions were anything but rational. I was triggered. Nothing made sense.

Then I mentally shook myself. *No, you are not going to die. You are going to get home and get back to your kids. You are going to keep fucking going, whatever it takes.*

When we finally landed, the flight attendant got on the PA system and made an emotional statement. "I know many of you on this flight experienced horrific things last night. And on behalf of the entire flight crew, we are so sorry. We're thinking of you and hoping for healing."

That was the first voice I'd heard displaying genuine understanding. She wasn't pretending it hadn't happened. She acknowledged it and simply said she was sorry and wished us well. They were the perfect words for the moment. And even though I wasn't nearly prepared to acknowledge what we had been through, in retrospect that was the first indication that I wasn't just going to fly away from that night and go back to my familiar life.

I didn't know it then, but my life as I had known it before the previous night . . . well, it no longer existed.

THAT WAS THEN . . .

Before the events of October 1, 2017, life seemed simpler.

I was—and still strive to be—a kind, grounded person. My family is extremely loving, encouraging, and open. I was blessed and am grateful for my upbringing and the family I created with my husband and three amazing children. My life was wonderful. And it was safe.

I was raised in a small town in southeastern Minnesota. My husband and I were owners of a family business where I spent my time as, first, the marketing manager, and then human resources director. This environment was where I discovered I had a passion for supporting others.

In 2016 I walked into my husband's office and asked what he thought about me getting my professional coaching certification. Business coaching was a bit of a foreign concept in the Midwest at that time, but I could clearly see the value and was thirsty to learn more. Together we decided that I would enroll in a two-year executive coaching certification program backed by the International Coaching Federation.

This was the beginning of a new life for me—a new way to view myself and the world around me. What I could not know at the time was that the skills I had been taught would not be used solely to support others in their careers, but would be applied to my own life after being involved in what is, as of the writing of this book, still the largest mass shooting in American history.

In fact, four days before the shooting, I flew back home to Minnesota after a weeklong in-person coaching deep dive in Boulder, Colorado. I was super excited and had all this new information swirling in my head. After my late flight I returned home to an empty house as my family was out camping. I sat on our backyard deck, looked up at the sky, and asked, "How am I going to utilize all these new tools to make a difference in the world?" The question seemed daunting.

In the darkness and chaos on the night of the shooting—again, this is just four days later that I'm realizing this—I had a moment of clarity. God was responding, and He was telling me exactly how I was going to make an impact. At that moment, my purpose became crystal clear. I remember thinking, *Oh shit, Krista—you asked the question. God is answering. "I hear you!"* There was a moment while I was running that I remember praying and begging for another chance at life. I just wanted, so badly, to get home to my kids. I remembered upon saying goodbye to the kids, before leaving for the trip, that I had kissed my youngest daughter's cheek and promised her we would wake her up the night we got home. I clearly remember, as I ran through the darkness that night, the pain in my heart, worrying that I was going to have to break that promise for myself, or that her father might.

In the darkness and chaos on the night of the shooting—again, this is just four days later that I'm realizing this—I had a moment of clarity. God was responding, and He was telling me exactly how I was going to make an impact.

After that night, I would never be the same person I once was. Somewhere along my path of healing and recovery, I had entered two words in my calendar for the date of October 1, 2017: "Life changed." Now, every year on that date, those two words appear on my calendar. I don't know at what point I entered those words, but they could not be more true.

Yet I also found myself stuck.

I knew that what we had been through was not normal—and I was responding to that, physically and emotionally. I wasn't sleeping. I didn't want to go out in public because I was paranoid that people were talking about me and judging me. I was scared to turn the lights off at night, and I hated silence, because when it was dark and silent I could still hear the sound of those gunshots. The news stations ran story after story about the shooting, all of it retriggering the trauma of that night.

I took some time off work and began doing what I called "investigative research," but this was actually just an excuse to watch every report from Las Vegas, to read all the stories, looking for answers as to why this happened and how we could keep from feeling so out of control ever again.

When I got together with the friends who had been there with us, we talked about those events, trying to process what we had all been through. We tried to find some connection, to unite and heal through this . . . but healing was not coming for me. I found myself isolating more, even from those friends.

I needed help. Yet as I reached out, I couldn't find anyone to support me. Therapists in the area didn't have appointments for weeks or even months out. I was terrified that I would end up in a psychiatric ward because I was so scared, so triggered all the time. I thought I might go crazy trying to figure out how to process this, that I might not come out the other side. I told Chris that maybe I should admit myself so I could get immediate care.

One day I was in the parking lot of our local grocery store when I heard the eerily familiar *pop-pop-pop* sound that haunted my nightmares. I immediately fell to the ground next to my shopping cart full of groceries, taking cover behind a parked car. Then I looked up and saw a medical helicopter from a nearby hospital, flying its routine, daily flight path. That was the last straw. I needed help, and I needed it now.

A friend connected me with a somatic therapist, and he helped me start to release the post-traumatic stress disorder from my body. As I was healing, in the months after I got back, I began to forgive myself. I got the support I needed to navigate what I was going through. I began to realize I was ready to share my story with others, to figure out how to help them walk through whatever they were navigating in their world. I had taken solace in my coaching, and with my newfound tools I was able to bring my skills to a deeper level. I was no longer just talking the talk. I was walking the walk.

Just as I had done that fateful night, to get unstuck from my past life, I had to choose to keep fucking going.

. . . THIS IS NOW

No one is more surprised than I am that I have a book titled *Keep F*!#ing Going*. I'm a speaker, coach, and leader of an organization. I don't use foul language regularly. I never even wanted to write a book—I'm a storyteller, not an author—but once I began writing my story, I realized no other title would work.

> The shooter's goal that night was to take as many lives as possible. Ultimately, however, his actions did not break me.

The shooter's goal that night was to take as many lives as possible. There were twenty-two thousand in the audience. He killed fifty-nine of those people and shot or injured more than eight hundred others. Ultimately, however, his actions did not break me. In fact, the evil acts of that night only ignited the fire within me to do the exact opposite of what he intended. He wanted to destroy as many lives as possible, but I was going to rewrite the script, flip the narrative, and make it my mission to utilize the tools I had acquired and positively impact as many lives as possible.

I even named my coaching business KFG Coaching, which stands for Keep Fucking Going—the thought that just *would not stop* running through my head as I ran from those gunshots. I had to keep going, I had to run, I had to get home to my kids—I had to *keep fucking going.*

As I've moved forward with my coaching, I've removed the profanity and shortened it to KFG, and that has become my mantra and the action step for my life.

You may have read my story and thought it was dark, scary, and ugly—and it was. But it also changed my life. It became a gift because I learned how to live and lead in a different way. It shook me awake. I was coasting through life on cruise control before it happened, but this awful night made me realize that I don't want to just have an okay life—I want to have a freaking amazing life. To do that requires that I KFG every single day and hold myself accountable, because no one else is going to do it for me. (Nor are they supposed to!)

I am so grateful that I get to choose every day to live a better, more authentic life—and now I want to help you with the tools to do the same in your life. This book is going to teach you the lessons I learned through this gift. I'm going to show you how to live in a different way, how to step into that vulnerability as you navigate through the unexpected events of life, just as I did—just as we *all* will.

You may be experiencing something outside your control right now. Perhaps you are short-staffed in your organization and wondering how to KFG through long days with seemingly no help and no end in sight. Or you may not have received the promotion you've been striving for and grinding toward, and you're wondering how to KFG when it doesn't seem worth it. If you are the leader of an organization, you may have realized that the higher you climb that corporate ladder, the louder your inner critic's voice becomes. How can you KFG with that voice in your head? What if you're a new parent? How do you KFG when you're exhausted and overwhelmed?

At times people come up to me and say, "Krista, I'm navigating a diagnosis, and the way you talk about processing the mass shooting, it was like you were speaking to everything I'm going through."

If you're navigating a divorce, a diagnosis, some wild unforeseen success, or maybe just your inner critic, guess what? I am too. I see you. I feel you. I am you. I have done it, and I am currently doing it—because I'm still living.

But here's the catch! You don't have to go through something like a mass shooting to come to the realization that you deserve the best life you can get. In fact, you don't even have to wait for the next life-changing event to take place to keep carving out the path to your best life. You can act *now*.

Whether you're navigating life's difficult moments or seeking to keep your foot on the pedal of your growing success, you have access to everything you need. Don't give up on yourself. Don't ever give up. That's the action step to all our lives: you have to keep going, through every moment, every change, every unplanned event that comes your way.

You just have to *KFG*.

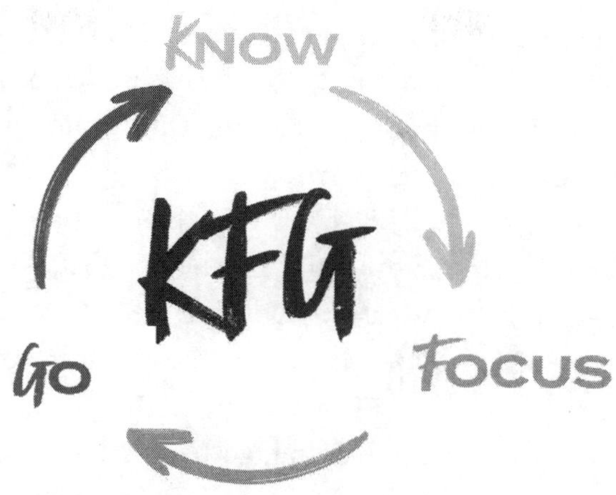

WHAT IS THE KFG FORMULA?

In the pages to come, you are going to learn clear action steps to support living your best version of you: the KFG Formula. And the best part is you only need those three little letters to remember this:

Know: You have to first *know* where you are so you can figure out where you're going.

Focus: Next, *focus* on determining the next best step to take, the one needed to get you from where you are now to where you want to be.

Go: Finally, take action and *go*—take that step toward who you want to become.

Know. Focus. Go. It's real. It's sticky and easy to remember. Just three steps. And if you follow these three steps, you'll see just how possible it really is to make a change and find the breakthrough moments in your life. You will live a better version of yourself.

Read through these book sections in the order they're written, because each section builds upon the ones that precede it. *K* doesn't come before *F* and *G* in the alphabet, but it does in KFG. You can't focus if you don't know where you are, and you certainly can't go if you haven't determined your next best step. Don't skip around, but do feel free to take notes and put stars or hearts in the margins. There are a lot of tools in these pages, so highlight information that resonates with where you are in *your* journey.

I'm providing this tool kit so you don't have to feel alone any longer. This is what worked for me—and maybe one piece of this book will work for you. If that's the case, it's worth it, because it's one more thing than you have when you feel lost. Read these words and know you are not alone.

And when you're done reading, go back to the beginning and reread this book (it's fairly short). The KFG Formula is like climbing a mountain. When you reach the top, it's time to start over—because you're actually at the base of a new mountain. And you are a different person, more equipped and skilled, because of the mountain you just finished climbing. KFG up this peak and the one beyond!

I want to be up front with you: this book is not a memoir of a mass shooting survivor. You now know the story of what happened to me. The remainder of this book involves we. Stories of others and how they KFG in their lives, the tools that have worked for them and so many others, the ways they have navigated change and found something better.

Let's do this! KFG: Know. Focus. Go. *And keep f*!#ing going!*

STEP ONE: KNOW

KNOW

AWARENESS

ACCOUNTABILITY

JAMES "J.R." REID

When James Reid ("J.R."), who grew up in Chicago, was thirteen, he started caddying for golfers at Medinah Country Club in metropolitan Chicago. Instead of sleeping until noon on weekends like most teens, he was up at four in the morning to be at the golf course. It was on Medinah's golf courses that he gained exposure and a sneak peek into the lives of high-achieving individuals: executives, entrepreneurs, and celebrities, including athletes and musicians like band members of Pink Floyd and Van Halen. He caddied for golfers for the next eight years.

Even at a young age, in addition to thinking, *I want to be like them when I grow up,* his thought was: *These are the people I want to help someday.* Little did he know that he would get this chance later in life, though not before overcoming obstacles similar to what many of these high-profile people face.

In college, J.R. played Division I baseball at the University of Iowa and drew a huge step closer to his personal athletic dream of playing professional baseball. A re-injury, though, would shut down that dream. So he shifted his focus to helping pro baseball players after college. He thought becoming a lawyer would be a great way to help these elite individuals, but his LSAT score wasn't high enough to get into law school.

It was time to pivot from his plan.

After college, J.R. moved to Phoenix, where he started working as a wealth manager at Morgan Stanley. Once again, he found himself surrounded by high-powered individuals and pro athletes. One of his first clients was a 17-year National Football League veteran. Their discussions began around finances but later evolved into conversations about life. Most people would look at this athlete and think he had everything—an amazing career, money, any car he could want—but he broke down in tears when telling J.R. about his failed relationships. There was a misalignment between his outward appearance and what was truly going on internally.

In 2008, after three years helping entrepreneurs and athletes on their businesses and finances, J.R. had a flashback to his caddying days and realized that helping these high-powered people in business and finances wasn't enough. He wanted to go deeper with them. So he decided to go back to school to earn his MBA and J.D. But J.R. wasn't content with just any school. He attended Louisiana State University so he could help its standout student-athletes transition into professional sports with a solid foundation of skills and knowledge about health, wealth, and relationships.

After earning his degrees in 2013 and helping several first-round draft picks transition to pro baseball, J.R. moved his family back to Chicago where he accepted a position as an attorney and agent with a major sports agency. Accepting that position seemed like the perfect fit for carrying out his dream. In that role, just as when he was a caddy, J.R. had access to the players he wanted to serve. But this time around, he actually had the skills, experience, and training to serve them at a high level.

However, within the first three months of employment, J.R. knew he was in the wrong place and working with the wrong people. It was a complete misalignment with his values and vision. As he put it, "They just wanted my Rolodex." Sadly, he didn't have the courage to tell his wife he was miserable, so he bottled everything up. He didn't want to disappoint her after all the hard work and sacrifices they had made to get to that position. J.R. felt like a failure, but he talked himself into "just pushing through."

J.R. knew he was in the wrong place and working with the wrong people. It was a complete misalignment with his values and vision. As he put it, "They just wanted my Rolodex."

So J.R. put his head down and went to work. He traveled four to five days a week, every week, for nearly four years. His routine when he got off the plane: go to the first grocery store he could find and buy a bottle of whiskey. At night, after dragging himself through the toxic environment he was in, he would drink himself to sleep in his hotel room. On the days he was home, he was disengaged from his wife and kids and gave in to self-sabotaging behaviors and limiting beliefs. He was far from happy or fulfilled. But rather than being open and honest about everything with the people he loved, he kept shutting himself down and distancing himself.

J.R.'s turning point came in 2016. While he and his wife Jessica were driving on the Eisenhower Expressway into downtown Chicago, about half a mile from their exit, J.R. looked in his rearview mirror and saw a vehicle coming way too fast behind him. With typical Chicago traffic, there was nowhere for the car behind him to maneuver, so it went to pass J.R.'s vehicle on the right shoulder. J.R. glanced ahead and saw two cars pulled over on the very shoulder that the out-of-control driver was heading toward. Immediately, J.R. thought, *This madman is going to kill those innocent people!* But just as soon as he finished that thought, his car was hit on the rear passenger side and went spinning out of control at 70 miles per hour—from the far right lane to the far left lane, and back again, finally stopping on the right shoulder facing the opposite direction. Turns out, the driver behind him had stolen the car at gunpoint and was fleeing police. He had realized he was about to hit the cars on the shoulder, so he overcorrected back to his left and smashed into the right rear of J.R.'s car.

While his car was spinning out of control, J.R.'s life flashed before his eyes. He honestly thought he was going to die at that moment and never see his wife and kids again. But a miracle happened. He and his wife were alive and unhurt. However, all the hurt that J.R. bottled up for the past three years came exploding out of him—fear, anger, sadness, frustration, shame, guilt—and all of it pouring forth with a vengeance.

When he got to his hotel that night, J.R. dropped to his knees and cried for hours. He replayed everything that had happened. Not just with the accident, but in the past several years working as a miserable attorney and sports agent. After he calmed down and came to his senses, he realized he needed to make a move: for himself, his family, and his own sanity. So J.R. opened his computer and sent an email to the sports agency. J.R. fired himself with that one communication. He didn't quit. In his words: "I fired myself." It was his choice, and there was a ton of accountability attached to it.

The next morning, when he told his wife what he'd done, stunned, she asked, "Uhhh, okay. Now what's the backup plan?"

"There's no backup plan," he told her. "There's just the primary plan: our family, our marriage, our kids. If we get that right, everything else will fall into place."

From that night forward, J.R. got focused on where he was and where he wanted to go. Part of that included having a real and vulnerable conversation with his wife, exposing all his drinking, depression, and double life. He thought she would kick him out of the house, but that was part of the false narrative he'd been telling himself for years—it was an example of J.R. getting in his own way. Instead, J.R.'s wife put her arms around him and said, "We're going to get through this." Had J.R. not been able to push through his fear, fire himself from his job, and take a huge step to get real with his wife, he would still be stuck. But because he made those choices, held himself accountable to whatever consequences he'd have to face, and cleaned out all the cobwebs, J.R. was able to set himself up for something new.

From there, J.R. went on a deep dive into his personal journey, reading all he could, attending conferences, and finding mentorships with people who could help him dissect who he truly is. He got realigned with what he'd known about himself as a 13-year old caddy—that he wanted to impact others by serving them in a way that felt right to him. J.R. told himself, "The best is in you—you have the capabilities to move mountains. Not only does your wife and kids deserve this, the rest of the world does, too."

In 2017, J.R. moved his family once again, this time to Florida. He considered the move a fresh start for his family. From that time forward, J.R. became more open about sharing his journey with the executives and athletes he was around. He noticed that the more he shared, the more they opened up about their journeys. J.R. realized he was on to something, so he started a business to help elite individuals bridge the gap from achieving outward measures of elite success to truly feeling significant and fulfilled. That's J.R.'s passion: making a difference and helping people maximize their lives. After his experiences, he believes it's unacceptable to settle for the status quo.

Not long after his family's move to Florida, J.R. was yet again reminded of the importance of alignment. During a drive home in his wife's brand-new car, he noticed it pulling to the left on a straight, flat road. Something was clearly wrong, so J.R. took it back to the dealership to have it checked. After a few minutes in the dealer's shop, the mechanic told him, "The vehicle's alignment was off, but just slightly. Unfortunately, that's all it takes for the car to start pulling, which can eventually become a big problem."

As J.R. waited for the mechanic to realign the car, he thought about how that simple mechanical default applied to life. When we're not living in alignment with who we are—even if we're just a little off—we'll veer off course. When that happens, we can end up breaking down, or, even worse, hurting ourselves and others. The other reality: when we're misaligned, we have to work twice as hard to get back on track.

How many of us are navigating the world with a misalignment right now because we're so afraid of looking or feeling like a failure? The reality is that the only way you're a failure is if you can't push past the fear and take an honest look in the mirror to see where you are right now—*before* you even start to consider where you need to be.

How many of us are navigating the world with a misalignment right now because we're so afraid of looking or feeling like a failure?

KNOW WHERE YOU ARE

The first step of the KFG Formula is to *know* where you are—where in regard to how you're processing your life, your experiences, the moments that are currently happening to you, for you, around you. It's about being real with yourself and saying, "Here I am. There's something happening in my life that is not serving me, and I'm stuck." Or, simply, "I want something different out of my life."

We can break this step of knowing where you are, so you can ultimately determine where you want to be, into two pillars:

1. **Awareness**: First, become self-aware that your current reality is not the one you desire. You want a different outcome.
2. **Accountability**: Then, fully understand and agree that it is up to you to create something new. You have to do the work; no one else can do the push-ups for you. You have to put in the time and commitment to yourself.

Let's look at these two pillars in more detail.

AWARENESS

Awareness is about taking off the masks society forces us to wear: "don't cry," "don't show emotion," "stay strong," "smile through the pain." We're trained to fake it until we make it—to not show our true colors. But all that does is create false armor as we pretend everything is perfect—until we can't even be honest with ourselves. That is toxic positivity, and it's only through recognizing and becoming aware of its presence that it can be eradicated. Where in your life are you faking it? And what is the result of that falsehood? This can wear you out mentally, emotionally, and physically.

The subconscious holds onto false narratives. We know when we're faking it, even when we think the outside world can't tell. We know the secrets we hide, that we don't want exposed, and how they poison

It's like having a beautiful piece of Versace luggage . . . that you're using to carry around a load of bricks.

us—nobody else. Those skeletons in our closets hang there, taking up space, and we know they are there, even if we choose to not acknowledge them. It's like having a beautiful piece of Versace luggage . . . that you're using to carry around a load of bricks. Everyone looking at the outside thinks it's beautiful and awesome, but they don't know how heavy it is to carry.

So let's break that apart. First, be honest with yourself. Dump out that suitcase, lighten your burden, and acknowledge that you're sore, you're sad, you're struggling. Once you know where you are, you have the ability to go somewhere else, become something different. You can choose to lessen your load and stop carrying the weight.

Having awareness about where you are is about creating space to look at yourself and say, possibly for the first time, "This is not who I am. This is not who I want to be. This is who the world expects me to be, but guess what? That's not real. Here's who I actually *am*, my true, honest self."

When we see ducks on a pond, they seem to be floating along so peacefully and serenely—but if you look under the water, they're paddling their legs as hard as they can. Don't just examine what can only be seen above the waterline; what is happening underneath? Are you paddling so hard just to stay afloat, so everyone looks at you and thinks you're a calm duck, when under the surface you're freaking exhausted and feeling like you're about to go under?

It can be scary as hell to admit that you're not fine, that things are not okay, that your happy face has been fake. It requires being vulnerable, honest, transparent. But it's rare for anyone who is faking it to actually make it, and that's why this courageous first step is so necessary.

This first step is about creating a pause, about really knowing where you are, so you can start to become aware of where you want to be.

It can be scary as hell to admit that you're not fine, that things are not okay, that your happy face has been fake. It requires being vulnerable, honest, transparent.

Knowing where you are means asking yourself who you are, as a human being, as an individual. What is the impact you want to make on yourself, your life, and others? What is happening in your reality right now?

It's only by knowing where you are that you can figure out where you want to go and who you want to become. It's tempting to skip over this first step and go on to the next, but that will not work. You need to pause and reflect, look at your raw, naked self, and evaluate what's actually going on with you right now.

If you miss this most important step of KFG, you won't be able to keep f-ing going.

When you know where you are, however, you can start functioning at a different level. You will refuse to put on that fake mask because you know it's exhausting and toxic. It sabotages your success.

This first step requires courage and complete honesty with yourself.

I want to be realistic with you: this takes time and patience. It would be easy to say, "This chapter is going to teach you how to dump everything out of your suitcase so you can walk around with absolutely no weight," but that wouldn't be true. The weight of the world can be heavy at times, and I don't want to set you up with false expectations. Knowing where you are is only a starting point—but it's where you have to start.

KEITH FINDS HIS AWARENESS

"I don't even know why I'm here, Krista. I have no idea why I was told to have this conversation with you."

Keith was a sales manager at a major corporation, and he'd been working his way up the company ladder for about twenty years. His supervisor guided him to seek coaching from me after two direct reports had recently left the organization and, in their exit interviews, cited Keith as their primary reason for leaving.

"They said my management style was mean and aggressive," he told me when I asked about it. "Why the hell is everyone so soft?"

I asked him if he knew why they would feel that way. He said he didn't fully understand this, but when the pandemic hit and everyone started working remotely, he adopted a very casual way of speaking.

"It was a tough time, and I wanted to make it easy on my direct reports, so I started to communicate with them like I was their friend," Keith told me. "You know, like bar talk. I wanted to make sure they understood I was there for them."

But then, he said, one of his staff made a mistake and fell short on a major sale. "Quite frankly," he said, "I told them that they were an idiot for what they'd done."

I immediately called out that kind of language as "trigger tongue": not thinking before you speak. It's an unskillful and inflammatory response that often triggers an emotional reaction. I also pushed back on what he'd said about not knowing why he was in coaching.

"Are you really unaware of why we're having this conversation?" I asked.

Keith started laughing. "Okay, maybe not. Maybe that was a bit aggressive."

* * * * *

Keith's story is not unique. Most of us have some awareness of where we are. We just like pretending otherwise because we don't want to face the difficult truth that we don't like it or that we want to change.

Keith was trapped in the story he was telling himself, that the best way to connect with his direct reports was to treat them like buddies.

From his perspective, he was doing what he'd always done. The perspective of his direct reports was very different: the way he was showing up made them feel unsafe.

He chose to focus on the employees who left by holding this attitude: "I am who I am—they should know I'm just kidding." But that's not pausing in the moment to know where you are and the impact you're making on others. Worse, Keith hadn't stepped back to ask himself if this story was accurate or true. That management style might work for some people in some workplaces, but it clearly wasn't working for Keith—and he'd need to do some honest work to turn things around.

After some time, and after learning to slow down and take notice during certain moments, Keith started to see things through a different lens. He started to get curious. He began to make a shift from "Why can't they toughen up and take a joke?" to "What am I doing to contribute to the reality that employees are leaving?"

We confronted the fact that his actions were impacting his career, his relationships, and his life. Keith paused and reflected, ultimately realizing that the first story he was telling himself was, "I am a leader of my organization, a high performer, so I can treat people however I want, and they can just show up and do their damn jobs!"

The reality, however, is that he didn't have the right to treat people like junk and expect them to stay. Nor should they! If they value themselves and their worth, they will likely step outside of that toxic environment to search for what supports them better.

The first step to begin turning things around was for Keith to simply gain awareness of the situation. He needed to be truthful and honest with himself about his own role in contributing to the breakdown between him and those reporting to him. He needed to acknowledge that there was more he could do to reverse the situation by changing his behavior and showing up more effectively—and he did this by putting himself in the shoes of those working under him to fully understand how his language would be received. Keith quickly started to understand that he had blurred the lines between being the boss to his direct reports and being their friend. He became aware that something within his leadership style had to change—and he was ready to hold himself accountable for the work.

The result? Nine months later, Keith's trigger tongue had subsided and those working under him gave positive feedback about Keith as a manager. He knew where he was, and perhaps more importantly, he could see just how far he had come. Keith hadn't realized how much the story he was telling himself within the walls of his work environment could devalue his leadership ability—even with the best of intentions!

FIVE COMMENTS THAT LET YOU KNOW YOU'RE STUCK IN YOUR OWN STORY

While you work the first step of the KFG Formula, **Know**, you may find yourself stuck. This is very common, and you are in good company—I was stuck too.

How do you know if you're stuck at step one? Most commonly, you're aware that you want a different outcome than the one you are in. Congratulations, you have nailed Awareness, the first pillar! Where you may get stuck is in the accountability to do the work, or you may get stuck in your own story.

I hear five common phrases from people in this space as they become aware that they are stuck in their story and want a different reality. For many, this is the beginning of knowing where they are.

Have you found yourself saying—or thinking—any (or all) of these?

- "I'm tired of feeling this way," or, "I just want to feel better/I want something different."
- "I keep getting in my own way."
- "I'm having a hard time moving forward or getting motivated."
- "I'm burned out."
- "I just can't see a clear path."

These comments are strong indicators that you need to take a moment, pause, and reflect on your reality. And if you find yourself saying, "Hmm, that sounds like me" when you read one of these comments, guess what? You're in the right place!

KNOW WHERE YOU ARE: ACCOUNTABILITY

Although I am sharing stories of other people, as well as my own stories, I want to emphasize that this step is about knowing where you are and about your own awareness and self-reflection, not about being concerned with other people or how hard they are working. That is just a way to avoid looking at yourself. Accountability is the second key pillar in this first step of the KFG Formula.

One indicator that you are stuck in that avoidance is if you are focused on someone else's journey and deciding whether the way they're living their life is right or wrong. It's so much easier to focus on other people and how they should grow and change—but this is all about you. Your avoidance. Your acceptance. Your awareness. *Your accountability.*

Whether it's your spouse, friend, or someone who works under your leadership, their journey is none of your business. That can be a hard pill to swallow because society tells us (and we tell ourselves) that it's all our business, that we are in charge of everyone else's happiness. Nope, they are. You are only responsible for *you*.

Let's take two very different situations—on the surface. You could be the leader of an organization. Or, perhaps, just parenting young children. In either case, you may be thinking, "Well, it's my job to focus on other people and what they're doing right or wrong, because I have to manage—or parent—them." That's absolutely true—as long as you're still focusing on yourself first.

You have to examine your reality and know where you are now before you can help others. You will not be able to make the impact you want unless you are willing to do the hard work to identify your reality first. And you can't take care of others if you haven't taken care of yourself. You can't fill the bucket belonging to others with water if yours is empty. In fact, if you try—giving away your last few precious drops and telling yourself it's fine, it will rain again someday—you are still wearing that mask of false reality, and that will sabotage your future instead of helping you succeed.

How do I know? Well, after the Las Vegas events I told you about in the first section of this book, I began going to therapy. It was really supporting me, so I kept encouraging my husband, Chris, to reach out to therapy as well. In my mind, therapy wasn't optional—that was how I was navigating, so that was how Chris should be navigating too.

Chris told me, "I think I'm navigating this in a way that does support me. I feel great when I work out—that's my therapy."

But I still thought, *No, that's not enough.*

It took Croft Edwards, my own coach who has supported me since 2016—Croft is a trusted, outside observer—pointing out, "What gives you the right to decide how someone else lives or heals? You are avoiding your own journey by attaching yourself to everyone else." And, he explained, I was doing this before I could even begin to realize what I was doing. In my processing of that moment, I was focusing so much on my husband—his healing, his journey—that I was avoiding being realistic about where I was.

Because where I was . . . sucked. I was stuck. And worse yet, the choices I was making were keeping me there. I was the VIP guest at my own pity party, and I had crafted this perfect storm! I spent eight hours a day supporting others as a coach, then went home and worked some more, building my business, all to deflect looking at myself and where I was. I gave work my all because I felt so fulfilled in helping others, but I wasn't allowing myself the space to work on myself or holding myself accountable to make the changes in my life that I desired. I was the queen of avoidance, wearing a mask of support for others.

I was the queen of avoidance, wearing a mask of support for others.

I was avoiding the self-care I needed to tackle because I was still relying on everyone else to help me—my therapist, my coach, Chris. I created a false narrative in my mind that the only way was *my* way. Everyone should be doing everything I was doing, navigating the same way, so we could be in sync and aligned. Doing this, I thought, we would come out of all this trauma in the right way.

I was so wrong. I was having an energy crisis. My marriage was suffering. My family and kids were not getting the best version of me. And I was avoiding myself and the real work that needed to be done.

But by avoiding myself, I was sabotaging my own success. And that is a key indicator of being stuck: when you think you're doing all the hard work to focus on yourself, but you're actually avoiding yourself to the fullest. That is a false mask of strength you wear when you're really unraveling inside, projecting peace and calm, as though you have it all together, when below the water you're paddling as hard as you can.

I was on the verge of a breakdown, burning myself out, and pretending to be happy and fulfilled. I was acting positive, energetic, bubbly—but instead of "fake it 'til you make it," you can fake it until you break! I told myself I was doing self-care because I was doing what I was supposed to do—going to therapy, getting coaching, taking classes, building my business, making an impact on other people's careers. But I was doing all that to avoid the quiet moments where I would have to face myself and be in my own company.

Externally, I heard myself starting to use this vague self-description: "I'm fine. Work is fine." But that line means nothing, and it wasn't even true. Today when I hear the word "fine" from myself or others, it indicates there may be some space to dig deeper. "Fine" is an avoidance word. It can mean the exact opposite, and for me it did.

Today when I hear the word "fine" from myself or others, it indicates there may be some space to dig deeper.

Eventually, I realized that I didn't want to be "fine" or "okay." I didn't want to coast through life anymore. I did not want to be a victim in my own story. I aspire to be great. I want to feel great, and to embrace that feeling—not with other people, but with myself. I wanted to love my own company so much that I can stand firm on the ground and be solid in myself, not have to look at others to fulfill me, satisfy me, please me. I was finally ready to do the work.

That is the moment I took off my mask.

I had to get naked in the mirror, take it all off, and look at where I was breaking down, where I was my own worst enemy. How was I holding myself back from a better version of me? That's when I saw that I was stuck, and that I was choosing to stay there.

I also started to see some common themes emerge, which I can now identify as the four traps of being stuck:

- Experiencing **Automatic Negative Thoughts,** or **ANTs**
- Condoning and camouflaging unhealthy habits
- Blaming and complaining

- Fantasizing about an alternate life

Do any of these traps sound familiar to you?

In the next sections, we'll take a closer look at each, because when you become aware of these traps, you can work harder to avoid them. I'll also give you some exercises you can use if where you are isn't where you want to be. I call these exercises **Strategies of Success,** or **SOS**. Why SOS? Because when you are stuck in a trap, you need to raise a signal for help—and these exercises aim to give you actionable help you can implement during every stage of your journey. They are part of doing your reps, your work, and they will also become part of your success plan.

THE ANT TRAP

The first sign that I was stuck was that, whenever there was quiet, I was my own worst enemy. I was a Mean Girl, and my target was myself. The Mean Girl is vicious, ruthless, and relentless. No one else can see her, but she took control of my life. She was like a shadow that would show up and overtake my thoughts. The Mean Girl was in the driver's seat of my life for quite a while. I wasn't even sitting shotgun—I was in the trunk because I didn't know how to shut her up.

For me, Automatic Negative Thoughts—or ANTs—looked like beating myself up internally, thinking that I should be living my life differently, that I wasn't a good wife, that I wasn't there for my kids, that I didn't know if I was ever going to be successful or not.

One of my most frequent ANTs was "I'm not good enough." I thought I wasn't doing a good enough job as a wife, as a mom, as a daughter, as a friend, or as a teammate. I compared myself to others and worried that I was just not stacking up. As an example, I once found myself looking out the window and saw a family go by together on a bike ride. Immediately I thought, *Oh my God, I'm terrible. I haven't taken a bike ride with my family in a year.*

If someone walked their dog outside, I'd think, *I should walk my dog. I'm such a terrible dog owner!*

Another time, I saw a friend of mine building a business. While I was happy for her, I also couldn't help thinking, *She's doing such a good job, but I'm doing a terrible job.*

Anytime I saw anyone enjoying their life or experiencing success, I would immediately attach myself to what they were doing and say, "I'm not doing that, so I'm not doing a good job."

I was stuck in my ANT trap.

SOS: CHALLENGE THE NARRATIVE

Your first Strategy of Success is to challenge the narrative.

> This exercise was inspired by the book *Own Your Greatness* by Drs. Lisa and Richard Orbe-Austin. This book was huge for me. It's a deep dive into imposter syndrome, covering what it is, where it comes from, and why we tell ourselves these false stories.[1]

One of the things I learned to do to counter the ANTs was to challenge their existence by asking questions and getting curious. The first step to shutting up the Mean Girl's voice is to notice that it is there, that it's trying to tell you something.

The second step is to ask it a question with the goal of shutting it down. Basically, this comes down to considering: what is the evidence for and against the thought?

Let's say, for example, that you do a presentation at work and your inner Mean Girl is saying, *Everyone who saw that thinks it was just crap, and now I look like an idiot.*

Well, what's the evidence? Did people actually say or think that? What was the real, honest feedback you received?

Or, maybe your ANTs are telling you: *That presentation was so bad I'm going to be fired.*

But now you must think of the actual realities. Have people been fired in the past as a result of a single poor presentation? Is this thought benefiting or harming you?

When I started to look at the real evidence behind my ANTs, I realized that none of it was valid or true. I was feeding my Mean Girl and letting her eat at a buffet—and she was feeding me lies in return. I stopped having the knee-jerk reaction of, *I'm not doing that, so I must not be doing well.* Instead, I looked at what I really was doing. My family and I did other things together, even if we didn't go for bike rides very often. I had taken my dog for a walk that morning, and we would go again in the evening. I was happy for my friend, and I knew that my business was also doing well.

Now if I see a family on a bike ride, I think, *That's so sweet. They're having such a great time.* It makes me happy to see others happy.

By asking these questions and examining the evidence, you can start to shift the whole narrative. When you realize those thoughts are not real, there's so much freedom it's almost comical. Identify that the Mean Girl is creating this trap for you, and you can shut her down. To this day, when I hear the ANT whispers, I will say, out loud, "Knock it off! You're not taking the wheel. I'm not listening to you."

That immediately acknowledges I am aware a negative thought has crept in. It immediately acknowledges I have full control over the thought and that I can shift it. Who is in charge? The thinker or the thought? Challenging the narrative gets you back in the driver's seat so you can navigate where you want to go.

Who is in charge? The thinker or the thought? Challenging the narrative gets you back in the driver's seat so you can navigate where you want to go.

THE TOXIC HABIT TRAP

The second sign I was stuck was when I started condoning and camouflaging some unhealthy habits. I was staying up later, eating terribly, not getting any kind of movement, and having multiple drinks by myself. All of this only served to fuel the Mean Girl—she *wants* you to feed her multiple glasses of wine and listen to sad country music. This is where she thrives.

Then I excused my behavior by saying I'd had a hard time, so I was allowed a pity party once in a while. Or I worked hard today, so I deserved whatever so-called "treat" I wanted. I'm not talking about going out for a couple drinks to celebrate an occasion, or rewarding myself after an accomplishment. I'm talking about a pattern of doing the same self-sabotaging behavior over and over, choosing to be a victim of my situation, which only brought me down deeper.

And if anyone tried to call me out on these behaviors, I'd hide even more, try to cover them up better, wear my mask even higher.

The best advice I received while navigating this time in my life was, "What if you started from a place of curiosity?"

When we live from a place of curiosity about ourselves, then we ask questions like, "What is my internal narrative of my situation?"

If I'm telling myself that because my husband came home late from work, exhausted, it means he doesn't want to be home with me . . . is that actually true? No. In fact, it's ridiculous. (That's FEAR again—false evidence appearing real.)

When I started to live from a curious space, I didn't feel guilty. I didn't feel shame asking myself questions. I didn't put labels on myself, like, "Oh, you're just being crazy."

Instead, it allowed me to identify some big areas for improvement by changing the way I think about the situation. When I started to get more curious, that's when I was able to hear the Mean Girl. I could evaluate: *What is she saying—and how can I quiet her?*

For example, if I noticed I was staying up late, I might ask myself: "Is this going to be the best move for me to set myself up for success tomorrow? Or am I going to be tired and have a hard time getting out of bed?" Well, if I know I'm going to be tired the next day if I stay up and keep working, then I'm not going to feel guilty about going to bed now.

Do I need to pour another glass of wine right now? No. Why am I wanting to? Oh, it's because I just heard an Eric Church song and it made me sad. Is pouring another glass of wine going to make me happy? No, absolutely not. Maybe instead I'll go to bed, listen to some quiet music, and think of two things I'm grateful for before I fall asleep.

When I started to live through this curious space, I began to forgive myself for the toxic habits I had created. I thought I had been protecting myself, but in reality I was the weight holding myself down. I was the reason I was stuck.

SOS: THREE THINGS

If you're finding you have slid into a toxic habit pattern, this exercise can help you by reminding you of the value of your supportive habits and refreshing your memory of what results those habits can lead to.

Identify a time in your life when you felt fantastic—when you hit all your numbers, your marriage was strong and healthy, and you felt fulfilled and full of joy. Now write down three things that were happening during that time.

Maybe it was during the summer months, so the weather was great and you were outside a lot. Maybe you and your husband were going out on dates and watching movies together, spending quality time being present with each other. Or maybe your family was traveling a lot, seeing new things. Maybe you were getting really good sleep, consistently, for seven or eight hours a night, so you woke up feeling refreshed instead of stressed. Maybe you weren't sacrificing (or sabotaging) that by staying at the office an extra three to four hours.

The habits you had during the times in your life when you felt best are huge indicators for where you are now. Are any of those things happening now? The answer is almost always going to be no—because if you have those same strong, healthy habits, it's hard to also be stuck in a toxic trap.

It is part of the human experience to get lost along our journey. We're trained to climb to the top and be our best selves, but that path isn't a straight line, and it's easy to wander. After a while, you look back and think, *How did I get here?*

This exercise forces you to reflect on a time in your life where you didn't feel lost or confused so you can start reframing your life to get back toward that same feeling. It'll never be exactly the same as it was back then—it's always going to be a different version—but it brings to the surface the truth of how you got to where you are so you can be truly honest with yourself about how to get where you want to be.

SOS: CIRCLE OF ACCOUNTABILITY

A second way to get myself unstuck and identify more habits I had created that were holding me back was when I learned to start the **practice of non-negativity.**

Adding positives to your life can help you lead a better, healthier existence—but it can also add so much pressure. You already have more going on than you can handle, and now you have to incorporate yoga, walking, meditation, therapy, and all this self-care? How!? You only have so much time and energy in the day!

The power of non-negativity is that it doesn't add anything. Instead, it focuses on eliminating a few of the things you know are negative in your life, and this in turn gives you more space for positives already in place. It gives the positives more attention and power.

Let's use a field goal attempt in a football game as an example. If you are watching a football game and the kicker is heading onto the field for a field goal try, you find there are two types of cheering happening:

on one side, they are cheering loud for support, applauding the kicker. The other side is booing and trying to create a distraction in hopes of the kicker missing. The power of non-negativity works by eliminating the "booers," which automatically intensifies the sound of the supportive cheering. You don't even have to add more people cheering—you just have to eliminate the negative noise, and the positive items in place will automatically intensify.

As an example of non-negativity, the exercise I like to do is something I call the Circle of Accountability. Let's walk through it using your morning routine as an example. How can you figure out a way to set yourself up for success in your morning routine?

First, take a piece of paper and draw a circle at the top. Inside the circle, write "Morning Routine."

Now here's where you have to be really freaking, ruthlessly honest with yourself—no lies, no false realities. What's the first thing you do in the morning when your alarm goes off? Maybe, if you're being honest, you hit snooze. If so, then draw a bubble under Morning Routine and write the word "Snooze."

What's the next thing you do in the morning? When I took my daughter through this exercise, she said, "I hit snooze again!" In that case—no judgment—her second bubble would also say "Snooze." What's the third thing? Maybe it's checking your phone—if so, write that down. Maybe it's going to the bathroom; write that as well.

Keep adding bubbles to your morning routine—go downstairs, make breakfast, eat breakfast, take a shower, get dressed, brush hair, pack a bag, feel rushed—while being open and honest until you've listed everything you do from when you wake up until when you leave the house.

Once you have all your bubbles listed, go through and put a plus sign next to the ones that help you in the morning. Going to the bathroom? Definitely a plus. Getting dressed, taking the dog out, packing your bag—these are all things that have to happen, that help you feel like you're making an impact and taking care of yourself. They all get a plus sign.

Then go through and put a minus sign next to the things you would attach as negative, that aren't helping you set yourself up for success. Maybe that's hitting snooze the second or third time if it makes you late or feel rushed. Maybe you decide that checking your phone is actually a negative because you get sucked into social media and it doesn't always make you feel great, or you start checking your emails right away, which gives you anxiety.

Finally, once you have all the pluses and minuses established for your morning routine, ask yourself: *if I had to eliminate just one bubble that would free up a little bit of space and help my morning routine be more successful, which would I eliminate?*

When I asked my daughter this question, she said, "I would eliminate hitting snooze the second time. I would still allow myself one snooze as long as I can hold myself accountable. And I wouldn't check my phone unless everything else gets done and I have extra time so I'm calm and ready for the day."

When you do this, it doesn't add anything—even any positives. You don't have to allow yourself extra time or build in going for a walk. All you have to do is work out a simple way to eliminate a negative, something that is honestly not benefiting your life.

If you can just remove that one little piece, you're starting to be real with yourself about how you're actually sabotaging your own success in very minor ways—but ways that all add up. You're also starting the process without making it feel unobtainable and impossible. The bubble you change for any of these doesn't have to be something big; start small.

And you don't have to do this only for your morning routine; that's just an easy example to start with. You can practice the Circle of Accountability for your success at work, how to be a more impactful spouse or parent, and any number of other things.

> If you'd like to read a more in-depth discussion of this topic, *Atomic Habits*, by James Clear, is a fantastic book that looks at ways to break bad habits and build positive ones by adding small wins or subtracting the small things that don't serve you.

THE BLAME AND COMPLAIN TRAP

The third sign that I was stuck was when I started blaming everyone and everything around me to avoid taking any accountability to act differently or even think differently. I complained about the stupidest stuff: I'm not happy because it's cold outside. . . . It's raining. . . . The kids were late for school today. . . . My husband didn't do the dishes. I made my choices, but then I wanted to complain about them too, about how much I was working, how little I was sleeping, how overcommitted I was.

Blaming and complaining announces to the world that you have zero self-accountability because you have a choice to do something differently about everything you're complaining about. You have a choice to respond differently, and when you choose not to, it shows a lack of accountability. It's a terrible habit that breaks down trust. When people hear you blaming and complaining, it's a red flag that you are not the leader of your own life or that you don't have the ability to handle yourself in any situation. In the workplace, it says that you are not trustworthy and don't have consideration for others because you don't talk to them directly. You want to stay the same instead of doing the work to make something better.

Blaming and complaining is the lazy way to avoid change. Stop complaining. Stop blaming. Just stop. No one wants to hear it, and the law of attraction proves you will get more of what you are complaining about once you say it out loud.

Sometimes our complaints can sound like dramatic storytelling. These comments may sound like this: "My boss loaded me full of work, and now I have to stay late." Or, "I am slammed at work. I feel like I'm running around on fire and constantly drinking out of a fire hose." By adding the dramatic language, we are actually digging the hole deeper and allowing ourselves permission to stay in the rabbit hole.

By acknowledging this dramatic language, however, we can strip it away. Furthermore, clearly defining our reality will support our remaining accountable and avoid the temptation to complain, blame, and add drama.

What if we strip the drama from our language? What if, instead of "I am slammed at work," we look for truth? "I have an important project that requires my immediate attention." Instead of, "I feel like I am running around on fire," we are accountable with, "I notice I have a lot of high-pressure projects I am trying to manage. I wonder who could support me?" By stripping the drama out of our language, we can support ourselves in shifting from being the victim of our reality to taking accountability.

SOS: GET A VERBAL VENT PARTNER

Karen is the senior staff editor at a large magazine distribution company. She reached out for support, telling me that she was "burning the midnight oil at both ends" and could feel herself burning out. Not only were her job responsibilities time-sensitive, high pressure, and high stress, she was also a working mother with a nine-month-old at home. And since the Covid pandemic, her office was also located in her home.

The first time we spoke, Karen had a lot to say.

"How do people do this?" she asked me. "I have no idea how I am ever going to make this work. My boss has such high expectations for me, yet I never know if I am doing a good enough job."

And: "I work such long hours, and no one even acknowledges the hard work I put into each story."

Still more: "I have to go cover the Oscars tonight, and I have absolutely no desire to even get dressed up to go out of the house."

And still more: "My little girl was up all night crying because I think she has another ear infection."

Karen went on and on and on, doing what I call "verbal venting." This is when you have so bottled up an internal narrative that you're having a full-blown pity party for yourself within your mind. Once you finally allow yourself a release, it's like verbal diarrhea.

I gave Karen all the space she needed to talk through all the stress swirling around within her. When she was done speaking, she paused, then started to laugh. "Wow, I've been rambling nonstop for twenty minutes. That was a whole lot of baggage I just unpacked. And when I hear myself saying it out loud, it is a bit silly."

Silly? Maybe. Human? Absolutely! You see, we all have moments when we get caught up in our emotional whirlwind. The difference between supporting yourself and sabotaging yourself, however, lies with whom you allow to be your verbal vent partner. It is perfectly natural to allow yourself a verbal vent, but you must be aware and intentional about whom it is you are venting to. For all the leaders reading this, your verbal vent partners are not your direct reports! For employees, your verbal vent partner is not your team member. If you are looked at as the person within your team who is always complaining, you are discrediting yourself and sabotaging the trust others will have with you. Quite frankly, if you are complaining about the rain and how terrible the weather is, how are you supposed to handle a challenging client?

Your exercise is to identify your verbal vent partner. Your verbal vent partner should allow you space to release and vent, yet also call out your BS when it has gone on long enough. Get their permission to allow the space for you to vent, but also to hold you accountable for shifting and taking action. This person will not piggyback and agree and complain with you (that would be a toxic partnership). Instead, they will provide space without judgment, shame, or guilt, and they will challenge you to take action and create a new reality.

I have a few verbal vent partners in my life. For one, my husband. Chris will allow me space to process and whine, but he will also challenge me when it goes on long enough without me shifting to a different action. My second partner is my coach, Croft Edwards. He calls out my BS when I start down the path of complaining and playing the victim to myself.

Having someone who will allow you space to vent is self-care as long as you don't create a habit of being a complainer. Be aware of it. Be accountable. And, like Karen, realize the power of your words and that sometimes what we are complaining about—our job, our child, the rain—is something others would be praying for.

THE FANTASY TRAP

The final sign that I was stuck was when I started fantasizing about living a different life. *Maybe things would be different if I had a different job . . . If I didn't live in Minnesota. . . . If the weather was only different . . . If I looked different. . . . Maybe my life would be easier if I had a different spouse or if I just started over.* Everything I found myself fantasizing about was based on playing a comparison game: "I wish I had *their* life, *their* location, *their* job, *their* partner, *their* hairstyle."

I started to find all these fixes that were really about still avoiding myself, still looking externally for internal satisfaction. It was the golden glitter effect: maybe the grass really is greener somewhere else.

I wasn't alone in this. I have a lot of conversations with employees who are unhappy in their jobs and fantasizing about new ones. They look on LinkedIn and picture themselves working at a new place, something with all the amenities. They think those perks will make them happier, so they dream about what else is out there rather than looking at themselves and the reasons they are unfulfilled.

One of my biggest fantasies when I was a young parent was dreaming about the picture-perfect Christmases I would have with my children. I fantasized about baking and frosting cookies, decorating the tree, listening to Christmas music. I just knew we would create all these special moments, and it would be absolutely magical.

But fantasizing is just that—creating a fantasy. A fake idea of something that will never be.

The reality? The kids were often in tears. There were so many meltdowns! (Mine included!) They didn't want to frost the cookies; they wanted to eat them. The ornaments didn't sit sparkling on the tree; they were dropped and shattered. And my husband and I were too stressed out trying to create a fantasy to sing merry songs.

In a Christmas card photo one year, my youngest daughter was absolutely bawling, my son had his tongue out, and my middle daughter was dressed as a pretty princess—but she was annoyed and scowling with her arms folded across her chest. I sent that card out anyway, with this inscription on the front: "Are the holidays over yet?" (I have to be honest—it's still my favorite Christmas card.)

It's only now that I can see fantasies are always false.

So how can we look at our reality and see it as our dream, as the place we're supposed to be?

SOS: AN ATTITUDE OF GRATITUDE

What can you do when you find yourself stuck in a fantasy? I learned to navigate through this stage of being stuck with one impactful practice: the attitude of gratitude.

This starts with awareness. If I start fantasizing about quitting my job and moving away from Minnesota, I ask myself where I'd go. Florida? Open a little slushy stand on the beach? (You may laugh, but at one point this was my ultimate fantasy.) Life would be easier then.

Life would be slower. I would be happier . . . wouldn't I?? Do I actually want to go?

Hell no. I'd miss my parents, family, and friends. I would miss skiing and our house. And guess what? I still wouldn't be any happier, because it was me I was not happy with, not my life, my job, my location, or my friends. And guess what? My fantasy involves me—I would still be there, still miserable, because it was the work on myself that needed a tune-up. Nothing less.

Once you have this awareness you can begin to speak your gratitude for all the reality in your life right now. You have many things around you to be grateful for: the air you breathe, the rain out your window, the warm cup of tea, the stranger walking on the street who smiled at you . . . look for these things and be grateful. These things are reality. Not fantasy.

Ask yourself: "What am I grateful for in my life right now?"

I started to break it down: why would I want to live somewhere different? I live in a beautiful home in a beautiful city I absolutely love. We've got a great yard with beautiful trees and room for our dog to run. I am actually one of those people who loves the snow, and my family and I love downhill skiing. I love getting outside and feeling that fresh, sharp air pouring into my lungs. The cold wakes up my body and reminds me I'm alive. I love my husband; he's been my best friend for more than twenty years. I have three kids who are absolute gifts. I can't imagine a better family. I'm so fortunate. When I show gratitude to God for the gift of my family, it lightens my heart and releases the tension of being stuck in the fantasy trap.

Once I started to look at what I actually had, I realized that if I had a different life, I would be praying for

Once I started to look at what I actually had, I realized that if I had a different life, I would be praying for the one I have right now.

the one I have right now. That's when I realized that thinking I would be happier if I had something different is a false illusion. Everything around me is a gift—as long as I can see it that way.

How are you holding yourself accountable for finding joy and fulfillment in your life, right now, with what you have in front of you?

When we're stuck, we only end up looking at all the toxic things in our lives. Instead, challenge that thinking and go looking for gratitude in this exact moment in which you're living, because when you decide you want to find something, that's what starts showing up. It's like when you're shopping for a new car and decide what kind of car you want. All of a sudden you start seeing that car everywhere! That's just how our brains work.

So start looking for the things you're grateful for—actively looking for and acknowledging them when they're in front of you—because it almost guarantees that more of those great things will start showing up.

YOU CAN BE SUCCESSFUL AND STILL GET STUCK

You now know the four main traps that can keep you stuck as you start to determine where you are. But it's incredibly important to reevaluate and continue knowing where you are, even when you've found success, professionally or personally, because it is quite possible to be successful and still be stuck.

One of my clients, Peter, is the COO of a large pharmaceutical company. He and his team have seen his business grow quickly; they've experienced tremendous success. Peter has been an effective communicator as a leader—he's vulnerable, courageous, and shows his appreciation for his amazing team. He's hitting all the marks you would want in a key leader of an organization.

But Peter came to me because he feels stuck. He told me, "Krista, I've been working so hard, and I never could have imagined that all my wildest dreams would come true like this. In just four years I'm exactly where I dreamed of being. I have a solid team, we're growing faster than anticipated, and I'm living the best life with a happy family. Most people would pray for the life I'm living—but the faster we grow, the more opportunities we see, the more wins we rack up, the more my desire intensifies to make sure we stay on this path. I know that's not a realistic expectation because at some point it's going to slow down and level out, and I'm scared to death of when that happens."

He was living in bliss, but it was a temporary bliss because he knew it could not last forever. (This is the nature of bliss!)

As we talked, Peter expressed that as his company was growing, the balance between work and home was getting blurred and his home life suffered. His professional success came at the expense of his personal life. Peter's family was supportive and loving, but he was actively choosing to work longer hours, hold weekend meetings, and stay in the office on Sundays instead of spending time with his wife and children. He wasn't experiencing burnout; in fact, it was the opposite: he kept pouring more and more fuel on the fire because his company was changing the world. Peter thought he was justified in making these choices because he wanted to maintain the level of success the company was experiencing so it could continue having the same impact on its customers.

To really know where he was, Peter had to balance his bliss with the reality of the world. Things wouldn't continue to grow at this pace—nor would they experience this business ecstasy—forever. And without finding some balance now, what would he have left once things started to shift?

As Peter's story illustrates, a breakdown doesn't have to be a traumatic event. Even when you're dominating, you have to be aware of where you are. Many organizations navigate the KFG Formula when they are in their most blissful moment. You still need to know what is really taking place each day so you can look ahead for creative solutions, keep your foot on the gas, and identify the best way to move forward in the moments of today—all to end up where you actually want to go.

NEVER STOP KNOWING

Lori came to me because she felt stressed, overworked, and burned out. She lost her father during the pandemic, and her Mean Girl was telling her that the people at her organization were judging her, saying she wasn't navigating the grief well, wasn't doing an adequate job, was dropping the ball, and wasn't meeting her quotas.

Because of those internal narratives, Lori was working extra hours. She was drinking so much coffee she got the shakes. She felt drained all the time. No energy. No motivation. No idea how to move forward. She was barely sleeping, she had no time for self-care, and every day she fantasized about working somewhere else, someplace where people didn't know her story.

She told herself: nobody understands me. They expect me to do all this work, and I'm not doing a good job. I'm so burned out, and they're not supporting me through mourning the loss of my father. They must not love me. I've worked here for twenty years, but I need to leave!

So we started to break it down and look at where she really was. First we looked at her ANTs to evaluate whether the things the inner critic voice was telling her were true. We took them one at a time:

- Will showing sadness and grief over losing your father make you look weak?
- Do you really not need anyone? Can you do this on your own? Do you honestly not want anyone in your life to support you right now?
- If you reach out for support, does this mean you've failed?

• Are you a bad employee? Do you want to quit?

One by one, we broke down the story that had been created. We pulled to the surface the truth and abolished the false tales that her inner critic had created to hold her under the water, creating a feeling very much like she was drowning.

We then looked into the daily habits she had surrounded herself with: minimal sleep. Minimal food. Many cups of coffee. Isolation from her husband and friends. Little physical activity.

When I asked Lori to work through the Three Things exercise, she easily identified what made her feel her best: seven hours of sleep, getting fresh air, and having relationships with those she loves (her husband, friends, and children).

"How are you doing with those three things?" I asked her.

"Terrible."

This was the starting point. This was the moment that, for the first time in a long time, Lori started to see that she was the only one holding herself back. She had created this armor of protection around herself, and it was suffocating. She wanted to take it off, to release some of the weight of carrying it around.

Working the Circle of Accountability, Lori created her first accountability action plan. She realized that having multiple cups of coffee during the day was giving her more anxiety, and it was also fooling her body into thinking it was not hungry, so she decided to eliminate one cup of coffee per day. At night before bed she often scrolled through social media, feeling sad while looking at the lives of others, comparing their happy faces with her own—grieving, lonely, tired—and yearning to be in a different place. So her next step: she decided to eliminate looking at her phone once she was in bed.

Slowly, Lori started to see the patterns she had created and the false stories she was holding onto. I remember one clear turning point in the KFG Formula for Lori. It was the day she told me: "I just realized how sad my father would be if he knew the time I was spending being hard on myself and sabotaging my life because of his passing. I can miss him and still be happy. I can create a new life and learn to love myself. I wonder if his passing can be used as a huge gift for me in learning how to live a new life—a really great one—while keeping his legacy alive through me?"

This was the moment Lori shifted. She stepped into a new idea, a new version of herself. This was the starting point for her. *What if . . . ?*

But here's the real secret: this process of knowing where you are never stops because we don't stay in the same spot. This is not a one-and-done. You can't look at where you are now and think that's where you're always going to be. If you see that your feet are stuck in that place, well, you've stopped growing.

If this happens, then you are going to come right back here and reevaluate where you are. You are going to remain honest and transparent with yourself. You'll likely trip up, but you'll still love yourself even if you have slid back into that "fake-it-'til-you-make-it" mindset or have started focusing on somebody else as a way to avoid looking at yourself.

If you find that happening, congratulations—you're on the right path. Tripping up—and becoming aware of it—means you're doing it right. And becoming aware and accountable is only the first step. Surround yourself with awareness as these moments of chaos and confusion are happening to you. Always bring that accountability to where you are so you can realize you have one or two bricks in your suitcase . . . and you can unload them before you get back to the place where you're carrying around a ton.

Bit by bit, those bricks will become stepping-stones that build the freedom to get you to the next step.

Before you move to the next step, however, I want you to ask yourself three questions. Be honest and truthful. This is your moment to be real and ready for stepping into a new version of yourself.

1. Are you **aware** of where you are right now?

2. Are you accepting full **accountability** for taking the action necessary toward becoming something different?
3. Are you ready to **claim control** over your own story?

If you answered yes to all three of these, you are ready for the next step. If you said no to any or all of them, that is okay! You're doing the hard work needed to prepare yourself. Go through and keep practicing the SOS tools provided so you can set yourself up for success.

When you have answered yes to all three questions, I urge you to move forward. You know where you are now, but how do you get where you want to be? What can you do to change your current reality?

KFG. Keep freaking going. Because the answers to those questions await you in Section 3 of this book.

Now let's recap the KFG Formula and the steps you'll need to break it down. When I lead discussion groups, I whiteboard the following. It's incredibly helpful to see it, and audiences can visually connect.

THE TWO PILLARS: AWARENESS AND ACCOUNTABILITY

Identify Your Traps:

- ANT (Automatic Negative Thoughts) Trap
- The Toxic Habit Trap
- The Blame and Complain Trap
- The Fantasy Trap

Use Your SOS (Strategies of Success) Tools:

- Challenge the Narrative
- Three Things Exercise
- Practice the Circle of Accountability
- Find a Verbal Vent Partner
- Gain an Attitude of Gratitude

Answer the three Questions to Move On:

1. Are you aware of where you are right now?
2. Are you accepting full accountability for taking the action necessary toward becoming something different?
3. Are you ready to claim control over your own story?

STEP TWO: FOCUS

JOSH LIFRAK

"We did it! We just won the World Series!"

As cheers burst out around him and people clapped him on the back and shoulders in celebration, Josh Lifrak paused and took a look around. It was 2016, and for five years he had worked with and for the Chicago Cubs of Major League Baseball as the team's mental performance coach. Now the Cubs had just won the World Series—for the first time in more than 100 years.

And in that moment, Josh realized it was time for him to move on—but he had no idea where to go next.

Because Josh wasn't sure what was in his future, he decided to take a look back.

In his late twenties, Josh had been a server in a high-end New York City restaurant. He worked a ton of hours, made a lot of money, and was very good at what he did—but all along he had an awareness that he was not honoring who he wanted to be.

The only problem—a dilemma he would face again, years later—was that he didn't know what the heck he wanted to do. He just knew that there was something more meant for him.

One day, as he was riding his mountain bike, he heard his usual mantra going through his head: "You can do this, you can do this." Josh wasn't just telling himself that he would make it up the next hill; he had been telling himself that he could get through this period of uncertainty. But now the mantra wasn't working. Instead, he shifted his mindset to look at the process: "If I want to get through this," he asked himself, "what do I need to do? How do I need to approach this to find success?"

That process of examining and shifting his mindset led Josh to his next step: he decided he wanted to go into sports psychology to help athletes find success through mindset shifts. He had been on a rowing team in college, and he had a sociology degree, but he hadn't previously worked in sports or psychology—he just had this aha moment that there was something there for him.

Josh went back to school, determined to show up as a good student and carry the habits and behaviors that would support his goal. He sat in the front row and took a ton of notes. He was knocking it out of the park, getting great grades, and was one class from getting his degree—except that one class wasn't offered at his college. He tried to enroll at another university, but was told the class was full. Instead of accepting that there was nothing he could do, Josh drove to the university, showed up at the professor's office, sat outside her door, and waited for her all day—until, finally, he was able to explain to her who he was and his goal of becoming a sports psychologist. Then he asked to be in her class. "I just need to get into this class, and I'm going to ace it," he told the professor.

She made an exception and let Josh in—and he overcame the last hurdle to get his degree.

From there, Josh applied for internships and was accepted at IMG Academy, which is huge in sports performance psychology—it's where all the big-name student-athletes attend. Sounds like bliss, right? Not really, considering he was thirty years old and engaged to his fiancé—but still sleeping on a bunk bed and waiting tables forty to fifty hours a week while also taking courses and completing this internship. Josh was fiercely focused on what he wanted, though, and determined to deal with whatever was directly in front of him. He knew that all of those obstacles were building blocks to get him where he wanted to be.

At IMG, Josh met Trevor Moawad, the guru of neutral thinking, who was working with top athletes as well as the best of the best in some of the finest corporations. Again, you would think Josh was killing it—except he was mainly making copies and stapling packets together. But he was also exposed to the craft, learning how Trevor related to athletes and put them first. Josh knew that when he had created enough of his own value, he would have a great deal of back end experience. He wouldn't be making copies forever.

And he wasn't. He was hired as mental performance coach for the Cubs to help support the organization's turnaround after a record 103 years without a World Series win. (That would stretch to 108 years by 2016.) They were known as baseball's most lovable losers, but Josh knew the organization would have to move away from thinking of itself as "cursed" or "doomed" to start showing up and acting like winners.

As you now know, that's exactly what happened. In Josh's fifth year with the team, the Cubs once again became World Series champions, winning a seventh and final game of a razor-thin World Series, defeating the Cleveland Indians.

That should have been one of the best moments of his life—and it was life-changing—but he realized that instead of living the high life, he was unsatisfied because the demands of that life meant sacrificing time with his family for time on the road with the team. He asked himself: *Am I going to stay in this baseball world that requires 250 percent of me, or am I going to choose to step back?*

After the Cubs' World Series win, Josh was asked to speak at events and for various organizations. At the end of one of those talks, a woman came up to him, crying. She said, "Your story is so beautiful. My mom was a lifelong Cubs fan, and I was just so happy she lived to see the Cubs win the World Series! I think if she'd known some of this mindset stuff you talked about, she might still be alive today."

That's when Josh realized the larger impact his mindset training could have—on more than one team or even one sport—while still allowing him to remain true to his commitment to his family, allowing him to show up and be present for them.

He joined forces with Limitless Minds, which Trevor Moawad cofounded with Russell Wilson, veteran NFL quarterback who has led the Seattle Seahawks, Denver Broncos, and Pittsburgh Steelers, Russell's brother HarrisonWilson, and friend D.J. Eidson. Josh works for Limitless Minds, a mental conditioning organization that unites personal growth with business success through the power of neutral thinking. (We'll get into, and define, neutral thinking in the third—"Go"—section of this book.)

Josh never lost sight of the fact that he was meant for something that would impact others. When I asked him if Limitless is his dream job, he said, "I don't know if it's my dream job or just a dream, because it's what I'm actually supposed to do. It's what I'm meant to do."

FOCUS ON YOUR NEXT BEST STEP

Josh already had the awareness and accountability that make up the pillars of Know—that's why he was able to walk away from his dream job and still be successful. But, he frequently tells people, he looks at life as a marathon. It's not just about getting over the finish line; life is a long journey. It can be daunting to look at where you want to go—and where you want to go today might change before you get there, so you never know where you'll end up. Instead, Josh guides people to look at where their feet are now, and then to think about taking the next step.

Similarly, once you have completed the first step of the KFG Formula, you have awareness of where you are, and you've taken accountability for the traps that may have kept you stuck there. Now, your burning question likely is: "I'm ready for a change, a different way to live. How do I figure out what my next best step is?"

This second step, Focus, consists of two pillars that will help you find success in determining your next best action. Those pillars:

1. **Values**: First, you must learn what your values are and determine whether you are in alignment with those values.
2. **Intention**: Then, using your values, you learn to live with intention instead of just letting life happen to you.

Let's take a closer look at each of these pillars, as well as the SOS exercises that will help you focus on your next best step. Even though you are no longer stuck in the traps we looked at in Section One of this book, I'm still going to call these exercises SOS because they remain strategies that will lead to your success!

ALIGN WITH YOUR VALUES

The first pillar of Focus is to align with your values.

Your values are your GPS for life, the compass points to help you navigate where you want to go. You first must be aligned with your values.

Don't be tempted to skip this pillar, because identifying your values is the yellow brick road you will follow to the Wizard of Oz (in this case, your next best step). If you start to navigate forward without first determining your values, you'll get knocked off your path. But as long as you're following your values, you'll make it to the Emerald City palace.

If you don't know what your values are, that's where you need to start—and if that's where you're starting from, don't feel bad about it. This is something I had never thought about, either. I had just attached my values to what other people told me. Things like: "Krista, you're so sweet. Everyone just loves you, and you're so kind to everyone."

All of that was nice to hear, but that's the way other people saw me, not necessarily how I saw myself (or how I wanted to see myself). Even worse, attaching my values to people telling me I was sweet and kind held me back from being courageous and speaking my truth because I didn't want to hurt anyone's feelings or challenge their idea of me as this sweet and kind person. I was just showing up as the world expected me to.

It wasn't until I determined I was in a place I did not want to be that I actually sat down and started to explore who I *am*.

It wasn't until I determined I was in a place I did not want to be that I actually sat down and started to explore who I *am*—not the mom, wife, daughter, friend, coworker, or coach that others might have defined me as—but who I am as defined through my values of joy, collaboration, and compassion. I started to understand that my values are not defined by anyone but myself, that they're what fill me up and make me the best version of myself.

Once I got clear on my values, I realized my GPS was not navigating in a way to support me at all. The times in my life I felt most stuck were when I was isolating, eliminating the true things that brought me joy in my life, and not having any compassion for myself or others. I was too stuck in my story to understand it was up to me to reset my internal GPS on my journey.

That's a place in which many of us find ourselves, and until we identify and start acting in alignment with our values, we can't take the next best step in the right direction.

In fact, the number one reason individuals come to me for an executive coaching conversation is because they're navigating a job challenge or change.

I had been coaching Michael for about a year and a half when he realized his time at his organization was up.

"I'm ready to move on," he told me. "I have two job offers, but I have no idea which one to take because they're both great, and I'd be really excited to work at either place."

My first question to him was, "Okay, so tell me, what are your values?"

"I don't know," Michael answered.

That's the first answer I get about 90 percent of the time.

"That's okay," I said. "Let's talk about what makes you feel fulfilled."

Right away, he started listing cookie-cutter ideas of fulfillment: happiness, love, gratitude.

"Let me stop you right there," I said. "Those are just words. I want you to tell me what makes you feel like your heart is singing and your blood is pumping, like you're perfectly warm inside and everything just feels right. Have you felt those moments in your job?"

"Oh yes," he said. "That's what it's like when I'm really busy in an office, working with others, when we're moving and shaking, laughing and collaborating together." As he went on, Michael painted a picture of his ideal work environment.

"You said you knew it was time to move on from your current job. Why is that?"

"Well," Michael said, "in the past nine months, I only see one or two people a day. We only go into the office once a week, and I just feel isolated. I'm lonely most of the day. We have a strong team, but we're not communicating. At best, we're just emailing back and forth."

From those two pictures he had painted—where he felt stuck, and where he had previously felt fulfilled and happy—Michael was able to connect the dots and pull out what was important to him: collaboration, connection, and face-to-face interaction with his colleagues.

With those three values in mind, I asked Michael to walk me through his two new job options. One was completely remote, with a team of four people who weren't even in the same state. The other was in the office every day. Because he had gained awareness of his values first, thinking intentionally and declaring what those values are so he could act in alignment, the choice became obvious. Michael was able to choose the job that would be both exciting and fulfilling. His GPS pointed him directly toward his next best step.

I'm not exaggerating when I say this is something I coach people on again and again. Another time, Angela, a C-suite (executive level in a company) leader who was killing her numbers, was unexpectedly let go when her company downsized.

"What am I going to do?" she asked me.

"What fulfills you?" I asked in return. "What fills you up and makes you happy?"

"Horseback riding," Angela said immediately. I was shocked; I had coached her for four months, and I had no idea horseback riding was even something she was interested in. Previously, she had been aligned with other people's ideas of success—working eighty-hour weeks, being on-call all the time, being the first in the office and the last to leave. Their values for her were that she be a powerhouse woman and badass boss. If she looked for a new job through that lens, she'd end up in a position similar to the one she just had—a job she thought she was supposed to do—but not the one she was *meant* to do.

"That's what I'm going to do," she continued. "I'm going to take my son and we're going to go horseback riding every afternoon."

She did that for a few weeks, and on one of our calls I asked, "So, what's fulfilling you lately?"

"It's really important for me to have enough time in my day for my family," she told me. "I never did that before—my job always took up the majority of my time, and it was so much pressure and stress that even when I was home I still didn't feel like I had enough time for everything. I thought my job fulfilled me, but I'm realizing it was the opposite. Getting let go was a gift—they actually let me *free*."

After that conversation, Angela realized that she would be more fulfilled in a part-time job so she could better split her time between being in the office and being with her family. She's never been happier—and she's still killing it with her numbers. She's just showing up in a different way because she's aligned with her values of nature and family. (I fully recognize that, for others, going to part-time may not be an option. But what might be an option is to move to a job with more reasonable, sustainable hours.)

If we're not aligned with our values, then we are not navigating effectively for ourselves and therefore can't possibly make an impact on others. Only where we are aligned with who we truly, authentically are—the best version of ourselves—can we impact others in a beneficial way.

SOS: LEGACY REVIEW

"Okay, Krista," you're likely saying. "That's all well and good—but how do I figure out what my values are so I can begin to align with them?"

There are three simple steps to identify your values. I call this a **legacy review**.

- First, identify a person who has made a huge impact on your life. This could be a family member, friend, coworker, mentor.
- Second, identify the qualities they displayed, and how they showed up to make such an impact on you.
- Third, have you considered that this person may reflect back to you your own values? Often, those who impact us the most are our mirrors. They left us with such an impact that we have woven them into our own legacy. And, fun fact: we are in the process of being that person for someone else. This is the "baton pass," like in a race. Living through your values impacts others and passes your lessons and legacy to those to come. What a gift!

Performing your legacy review will determine if you are living in alignment with your values.

These three answers are key indicators of your values.

Performing your legacy review will determine if you are living in alignment with your values. Here's another exercise: imagine you are no longer on this earth. If three to five people from your life who you were exposed to the most—not necessarily the people who knew you best, but maybe your boss, a coworker, or the neighbor who comes over a few times a week to walk your dog—were asked to stand in front of an audience during your celebration of life and speak honestly about who you were as a person, what would they say? If the words they would use are how you want to be remembered and what made you the best version of yourself, then you're probably aligned with your core values.

When I first performed this exercise for myself, I realized that, at the time, people would likely say I was sweet, always went with the flow, and got along with everyone. But that wasn't how I wanted to be remembered! The values that make me the best version of myself are joy and connection with a dose of courage—and those are the words

I would want someone to use when remembering me. A person sharing would say something like this: "Krista was filled with joy, deep into her soul, and we had the best, most thoughtful conversations. She thrived on connecting with the people around her and was not afraid to use her voice and speak up, even through conversations and discussions that others would see as complex." That would mean I'm living in alignment with my values.

If you're not aligned with your true values, you can start creating them or looking at what they are. Figure out your top two or three values that make you feel most fulfilled or closest to the truest, most authentic version of yourself—not who you think (or other people think) you are *supposed* to be, but who you *really* are. As long as you are aligned with those values, that security can help you navigate the rest of your day, week, year.

It's easy to get off track as we navigate our lives. Reminding yourself frequently of your values will help you stay the course. Today, I have mine written on my whiteboard. They remind me daily of who I am, of what makes me my best self.

> Your values might change over time. My previous top two values were joy and courage. When I was learning to step into who I wanted to become, I had to really lean into courage as one of my values. But now that I've been there a while, I've let go and realized that having courage is not as important in this moment as connecting with others. And that's okay. Your values will change over time because you're changing and growing as a person.

LIVE WITH INTENTION

The second pillar is to live with intention. Take a moment to pause and visualize yourself navigating whatever is ahead. Actually see yourself moving through it, visualizing yourself becoming a success, anchoring yourself in that intention. Before I get on stage, I set my intention: “I want to connect with the audience. I want to relate with them. I’m going to smile and have fun.” Then I see it happening, in my mind, because that starts to create the reality. My body and brain start to respond and think, *I’ve done this before. I can do it again.*

Living with intention is easy to say, but it can be very hard to do and hold yourself accountable to. My family and I recently took my son to tour prospective colleges. On the way home, we passed a park that we had driven by many, many times before on family trips to the lake, and I remembered how often we used to stop so the kids could go take a break and play. We would all pile out of the car to spin and swing and run around for a little while before getting back in the car and driving the rest of the way home. It was so much fun; I loved it. But driving by this park this time, staring out the window, it dawned on me that I never knew the last time we stopped at that park would be the last time. My kids are teenagers now, and we haven’t been to the park in years. Similarly, I never knew that the last time I read them a story out loud would be *the last story.* It just happens.

If I could go back and set a higher level of intention in those moments, I might have been able to lock them in as core moments. Now I seek to navigate my life with intention so I don’t miss out on another first or last moment.

A while back, I was given the opportunity to take one of my daughters to a Taylor Swift concert. She’s a huge fan of Taylor’s, so I knew this would be a core memory for her. I set the intention of being present for her and making it *her* night, connecting with her in a way that supported her, and just being open. During the concert I looked over at her dancing and singing along, and I was so fulfilled and happy in that moment. This was one of those moments where the rest of the world stopped. I was living *in it.* My intention had been born into reality through awareness and accountability. This is the power of living in each moment as if it was the only one that matters . . . because, really, it is.

505: SET YOUR INTENTIONS

Part of living with intention includes allowing the space and time to actually carve out intention. It's easy to do—but also easy to ignore. Ironically, you have to be intentional about setting your intentions!

So often we don't allow that space; we just show up and do whatever needs to get done. But when you start to pause and live with intention, it can provide so much more opportunity for success. Allow yourself a moment for a pause, a break in the day, and then take a deep breath. This pause creates space between knowing where you are and the action that takes place. It exists *here*, and now is in focus. In that space, you can enter intention.

When you wake in the morning, do you set a specific intention for the day? Or do you just try to make it to five o'clock when you can be done working? Those are two very different ways to start your morning—and they will lead to different outcomes for your day.

For example, if you're getting ready for a meeting, take a moment to find space before the meeting starts so you can set your intention. Ask yourself, "What would success look like in this moment? How can I lean into this meeting with joy, compassion, and connection?" (Those are my values, but you can insert yours so you are intentional about showing up with those values intact.)

Life goes so quickly, and we're often rapidly moving from one thing to another to another. If we're not careful, it can be easy to lose track of the power of living with intention. You may have conversations with coworkers or direct reports and realize, *I don't know if they even heard what I was saying.* Well, did you allow space beforehand to show up and carve out your intentions for the conversation? Was it your intention to show up as a supportive leader, to make sure they felt heard and understood, that everyone walks away feeling it was a successful conversation?

Intention setting is not about saying, "My goals for the year are X, Y, and Z." It's a moment-by-moment practice. Consider setting an intention for your morning, whether that's to eat breakfast, complete a couple of tasks, or go for a walk before you leave for work. Then set an intention for your workday: to go into that meeting with curiosity, to finish that project in the afternoon, to take some time for yourself during lunch.

It's not just about saying the words. Living with intention means acting toward the intentions you set. Many times managers and team leaders speak intentions but do not act through them, which can sabotage their success. For example, let's say a team leader decides to be intentional about personal boundaries, and the leader states to his/her team that they don't expect anyone to respond to emails after five o'clock. But if they then send emails or respond to them at seven that night, they're sabotaging the intention they have set. The team lacks clarity: has the intention been reset? Is it said that we should stop emailing at five, but the unspoken understanding is that we actually do something different? In this example, clear communication can reset the intention and rebuild trust: "I am going to respond to emails until eight at night because that frees up some of my time in the morning and gives you direction as to what to start on tomorrow. However, the intention for the team is still to turn off your computer at five and not respond until the next day."

And this doesn't have to stop at the workplace! Another common theme is that by the end of the day, we're exhausted. We're burned out, our tanks are empty, and then we come home to the people we love most—but we have the least to give to them. There is a lot of power in setting an intention before you walk in the door. Provide yourself that space, to say, "I'm about to walk into the house and see the people that mean the most in my life. My intention for when I walk in is to give them a hug, tell them I love them, ask about their day, and tell them about mine."

Intention setting can be quick and easy. Keep these two simple statements in your back pocket for setting your intention for moments of success.

1. "My intention for this moment is ___________."

2. "My intention for showing up for this individual is __________."

Feel free to fill in what you want to be intentional about—whatever is most important to you and your loved ones—and use your values to set an intention for success. When you become more intentional about your life, more opportunities unfold for you to see the next best step you can take.

> Pro tip! Share your intentions with others! They want to be part of your journey! Defining your intentions can help them understand you better, and they can support that intention becoming a success. This will also deepen the level of trust they have for you in that moment.

HUBERT PAYNE: LIVING WITH PURPOSE IS A SUPERPOWER

Hubert Payne is the drummer for the country music group Little Big Town. But his first love wasn't music—it was football.

Hubert grew up in Detroit, Michigan, the son of an elite drummer. Although he had the genetic makeup and the gift of music, Hubert's dad didn't want him to become a musician, so he never educated Hubert in music, never bought him drumsticks, and didn't teach him how to read music. Hubert enjoyed music and played around with the drums quietly at home, but he really wanted to play football.

His passion was so strong that Hubert went to an all-boys boarding school so he could focus exclusively on the game. After high school Hubert went to Saginaw Valley State University in Michigan to play college football. A bit later, the school actually eliminated his playing position, so he transferred to Tennessee where he finished his football career at Middle Tennessee State University. But he was crushed; his whole identity had been wrapped up in going pro. When he didn't get that opportunity, he panicked and was unsure of any other skill set that would ignite the fire that football did. He didn't know what to do from there. Football had been his identity for so long—and now nobody cared how fast he could run or how much he could lift.

Along his journey, Hubert was baptized in a Baptist church. Often when he walked into that church, he saw musicians, including a drummer, playing, and thought, *This is so inspiring.*

So Hubert started to play the drums for fun on Sundays during worship in his church. The original drummer for the church approached Hubert and said, "I feel like God's telling me that I'm getting in your way." And, just like that, he handed over his drumsticks. Hubert was aware that making a living as a professional drummer was possible due to his father's journey, but until he received his first paycheck, Hubert had no idea that playing in church was something people got paid for—that this could be a career.

His passion quickly became all about drumming, and he started playing at the church as much as possible. Then, at the age of 27, he realized he needed to take responsibility for his inspiration on this drumming journey. He needed to do more with his craft, with his musical ability, so he applied to the Los Angeles Music Academy. Hubert received a scholarship for the year-long program, and there he learned the ins and outs of music, slept on his uncle's couch, and ate a Honey Bun for lunch every single day. He saw other musicians struggle, and this opened his eyes to the cutthroat, competitive nature of the music industry. But he also realized he had a special gift—and the ability to take it to a higher level.

When Hubert returned to Nashville, he was on fire. He went to music venues with his friends to observe other musicians. One night in January 2010, at a going-away party for a friend, Hubert and his friends were hanging out after an event, trying to decide if they wanted to go to IHOP or Waffle House, when a guy walked in. It was January, so the man was wearing a big, bulky jacket—as pretty much everyone in the room was—but he was also holding a large can of beer and seemed to be distraught. The guy walked in, grabbed the microphone, and started rapping into it.

At first, everyone just watched him, but then he started swearing and yelling about how no one was listening to him. He reached into his pocket, pulled out a knife, and sliced the beer can, brandishing it as a weapon, and then started yelling directly into people's faces.

In that moment, Hubert felt a sense of responsibility. His football training came back to him, and he knew it was *go time*. He stepped up, and the guy held his knife to Hubert's temple. And, in that moment, Hubert . . . flashed back to watching *Mighty Morphin Power Rangers* with his brother as a kid. There was one episode where the Red Power Ranger was caught on his own in a goblin attack. The Power Ranger remained calm, and when the goblin wasn't expecting it, he side-swiped the goblin's arm and knocked him down. Since that day as a kid, Hubert knew that if he was ever caught in a similar situation, he would respond calmly, catch the threatening guy off guard, and disarm him.

Well, life isn't exactly like a cartoon. Hubert remained calm and got the guy's arm, but they struggled back and forth. He was able to knock the sliced beer can out of the guy's hand, but the assailant was still holding his knife. The guy kept trying to stab into his side, but Hubert's big winter jacket protected him . . . until he looked down and saw he'd been cut on his hand.

Hubert got away, ran outside, and flagged down a nearby police officer, who subdued the attacker. After all this, someone asked Hubert, "Where were you hit?"

He couldn't remember, and he didn't feel anything. He stared down at his hand and realized it was sliced all the way through. He also felt like he had wet his pants—but when he looked, the wetness was blood. He had been stabbed in his leg, deep, down to the femur.

In the emergency room, Hubert was told he needed emergency surgery on his hand. His tendons had been cut through on his pinky finger, which is like cutting through a rubber band. Instead of stretching and releasing, the tendons just wanted to bunch up, which would leave his hand paralyzed and unable to open. Fortunately, he told the surgeon how important drumming was to him, and the surgeon was able to repair Hubert's pinky. (It's still permanently curved, like a lowercase letter 'r'.) Following that surgery, he was told he would be able to hold a drumstick again someday.

He would physically recover—but he had to sell his drums to pay his medical bills. He also had to move in with his parents and sleep on their couch for a year. During rehab that year, Hubert had to start by picking up clay, then sand, learning how to use his hand, first in the most basic ways.

When he told me this, I asked, "Was that the hardest year of your life?"

He smiled and said, "That was the best year of my life!"

He performed some deep self-reflection, got vulnerable and honest with himself, and asked, "'What do I want moving forward, and what are my limiting beliefs?"

Through his introspection, Hubert learned that his ego had been wrapped up in being a football player, but he realized that if he took back his identity, he could still use what he had learned from the game—all the skills he had acquired, how to overcome adversity, personal development—for something bigger. He also realized that he had limiting beliefs about himself as an artist and country musician. As a Black man, he didn't think anyone would hire him. But he set about shifting his mindset to challenge those limiting beliefs.

Once he recovered from the surgeries, Hubert started going down to Broadway in Nashville, showing up at musical venues and bars, just to listen. He'd ask himself questions like: *Who do people like, and why? What makes them put a tip in that jar or ask for a certain song to be played?* He knew how to play music, but now he was studying the craft.

Hubert also learned that part of being a drummer is not just being a great musician, but also helping everyone else in the band sound great. As he figured out how to build up others around him more, he started to get more and more gigs, night after night, request after request. He became known as "the Broadway drummer," and this opened up even more opportunities for him.

Through one of those opportunities, he met his wife. They got married and had five children in nine years. After their second child was born, Hubert was in Las Vegas playing with a band when his wife called and told him they were expecting again. When he realized they'd be going from a family of four to a family of five, he decided that while he wanted to remain passionate about his music, he needed to do it at a more elite level. Hubert had to lean in big.

He'd recovered from being stabbed and gone on to play around the world with artists from all walks of life. He knew he could be bold, and he knew his worth.

Soon he got a call to audition to be drummer for Little Big Town. The band's drummer—who Hubert had reached out to years before, to ask questions of and learn how he had mastered his craft—was leaving the band for an opportunity to be drummer for country star Keith Urban. He'd put Hubert's name forward as a replacement, and when he auditioned, Hubert remembered his responsibility for his inspiration. He had a clear vision of what Little Big Town needed from a drummer, and he performed through that—to support the band and make it shine.

His life's purpose comes out in his music—and that is his superpower.

And he found that he really aligned with the other members of Little Big Town. They all had families. They didn't tour the world for hundreds of nights a year. Their intentions are extremely family-focused, and they've still been able to travel the world, win tons of awards, create eight albums, and perform for hundreds of thousands of people.

Hubert never allowed himself to fall backward into blaming and complaining, thinking his life was over because he'd hurt his drumming hand. In fact, he didn't fall into any of those traps. If he had, he likely would not be the amazing professional drummer he is today. Instead, he focused on what he could control, lived and played in line with his intentions, and worked to take the next best step for him.

* * * * *

Before you move to the next step, I want you to ask yourself three questions, as we did with the *Know* section. Be honest and truthful. This is your moment to be real and ready to step into a new version of you.

1. Are you aware and anchored in your values? If so, what are they?
2. Are they visible—somewhere you can see them every day?
3. What is your intention in this moment? Is it crystal clear?

It is only by navigating through your values that you can possibly reap the benefits of your life. And make sure they're visible, somewhere you can see them multiples times a day, every single day. We live in a fast-paced world, and it's easy to forget.

Sometimes people think, *Yeah, my values are family and love and commitment, and my intention is to love my family and stay committed to them.* No, no, no—this is way deeper than that! Take a clarity break and think about your values and the intentions you have so you can get ready to Go in Section Three of this book.

If you answered yes to these three questions, you're ready for the next step. If you said no to any or all of them, that's okay! You're doing the hard work needed to prepare yourself. Keep practicing the SOS tools provided and set yourself up for success.

When you have answered yes to all three questions, I urge you to move forward. You know where you are, and you are focused on your next best step.

But how do you get where you want to be?

All you need to do is KFG, keep freaking going, because Section Three will teach you how to Go.

THE TWO PILLARS: VALUES AND INTENTION

Use Your SOS (Strategies of Success) Tools:

- Legacy Review
- Intention Setting

A side note about the legacy review in case you see one of my presentations in person: I often do not do this SOS when speaking to corporations. I've learned that this creates way too many tears in the room! I do use this in retirement parties. However, I do recommend you do this exercise for yourself at this point! (I just don't do them in larger corporate-type settings.)

A note about values: often, these are the values that you see in others that you admire, think of, and want to emulate. Capturing this helps you produce these in your life. (Often, it's much easier to see the values you desire in someone else first rather than just calling them your values and seeking to make them stick.)

Answer the Three Questions to Move On:

1. Are you aware and anchored in your values? If so, what are they?
2. Are they visible—somewhere you can see them every day?
3. What is your intention in this moment? Is it crystal clear?

What Are Your Key Values?

List Them Here:

____

____

____

STEP THREE: GO

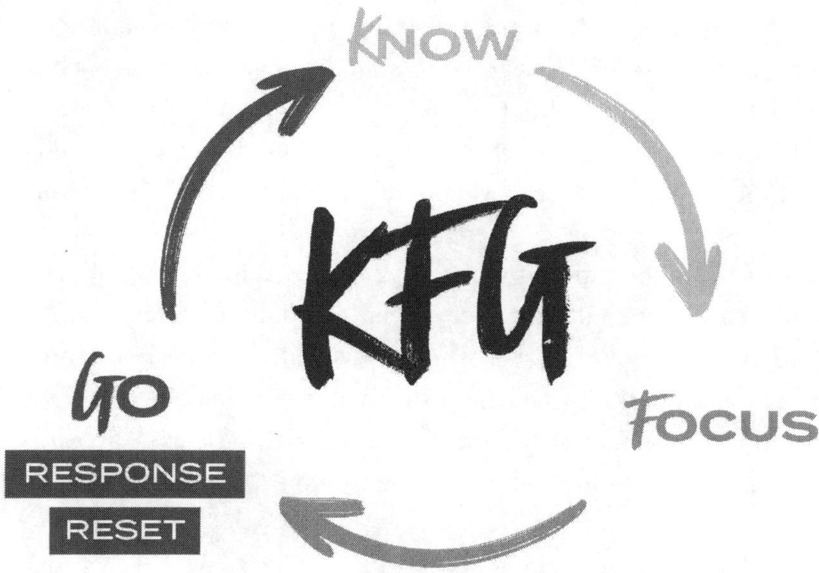

When I was 14, my Girl Scout troop spent the better part of a year selling Kirby Puckett candy bars, a fundraiser marketed with the name and image of a Hall of Fame player for the Minnesota Twins. Our goal was to earn enough money so the whole troop could take a trip to Maui. Talk about a BHAG (big hairy audacious goal)!

We sold the hell out of those candy bars, and we earned the amazing opportunity of going to Hawaii.

Finally, the day of the trip arrived, and we boarded a plane in Minneapolis bound for Los Angeles, where we would change planes before flying on to Honolulu. My friends and I all found our seats, and my mom—the troop leader—sat right behind me. The seat next to me remained open until a boy about my age made his way down the aisle and sat next to me. My face flamed with embarrassment. I was a teenage girl sitting next to a teenage boy. So awkward!

Before the plane left the gate, the boy started talking nonstop. He told me his name was Chad, the rest of his family was sitting at the back of the plane, and he was going to a Dodgers game in LA. As he chattered, he also giggled about all the pretty girls seated around him. When he asked me the name of the girl sitting across the aisle, I told him, and he wiggled his eyebrows up and down, saying, "Woo woo, Jody!"

Then, as the plane started to take off, he reached forward, grabbed the airsick bag, opened it right over my lap, and started violently gagging into it. I looked over, horrified, only to see him dissolve into more giggles. It was a prank! Immediately, I turned beet red again.

My mom leaned forward to check that everything was okay. She could tell I was uncomfortable, so she whispered, "Krista, look at his shirt."

I looked over at Chad, who was still grinning, and saw three words that changed everything.

Make-A-Wish.

"Tell me about your shirt," I said.

"I'm going on my wish," he told me. "I get to throw the first pitch at the Dodgers game!"

"Oh, wow, that's awesome!"

Then, very bluntly, he said it.

"I have terminal cancer. I'm going to die."

He continued talking, telling me his story—about all the surgeries and treatments he'd been through; how excited he was to throw out the first pitch at the game—and he was very matter-of-fact and funny.

I had never met someone with so much courage and vulnerability, the very definition of joy.

I had never met someone with so much courage and vulnerability, the very definition of joy.

A bit later, he said, "I hope people don't cry really hard after I pass away. I just want my family to be okay."

Then he looked at me and asked, "Do you think you would cry at my funeral?"

I had never considered something like that before, but I answered as honestly as I could. "I think I probably would," I said. "It's sad when someone you care about is no longer here."

He nodded, then grinned. "Just remember how cute and funny I am!"

Chad knew his disease was terminal, but he wasn't going to wallow in that. He had made his peace with it, and he wanted people to remember him with joy and happiness—that was the legacy he wanted to leave.

Chad was the first person I'd met who had been dealt such a difficult, unfair hand in life, but he treated every moment he had left like it was the best in his life. That ended up being a transformational moment for me, just witnessing his maturity. In his position, I would have been scared to death, curled up in a ball, crying.

With that one conversation, Chad changed my life. For the first time, I witnessed the power of choosing your own response to any given challenge or situation. I saw how one person, who is able to be vulnerable, courageous, and live through his values can make an impact to another that lasts a lifetime. Years later, I became a volunteer wish-granter for Make-A-Wish and went on to serve on the board for the Minnesota Make-A-Wish chapter and foundation. And I began to get curious about how someone in such a challenging situation was able to live with such joy.

Almost thirty years later, I am starting to understand his secret—neither of us could have known it at the time.

Chad was the embodiment of the KFG Formula.

GO TAKE THAT NEXT STEP

Once you are crystal clear on what your next best step is in this moment, how do you actually take that step?

I recently watched a video from Jocko Willink, an author, podcaster, and retired Navy SEAL, who has a one-word answer for how to take the next best step: *step*. That's it, that's the answer. *Just take the step.*

I found his answer powerful because it's so simple. We tend to overcomplicate absolutely everything, and that is so unnecessary. We know what the next best step is, but we've already created a million reasons why it can't happen, why it won't happen, why it won't be a success, *why, why, why*—anything to avoid actually taking the step.

Well, instead of leaning into those excuses, let's examine how you can actually just take the next step, using the two pillars of Go:

1. **Neutral**: Shifting to Neutral thinking is a high-performance strategy that emphasizes judgment-free thinking, especially under high pressure situations. (This is from the book *It Takes What It Takes* by Trevor Moawad.) Neutral thinking focuses on the facts without judgment or grading. It is where the truth lives, and where you can choose to carve out your next best step.
2. **Surrender and Reset**: Once you're in Neutral, let go of the end result, what you want to have happen, and surrender to what will be, allowing your life to happen. If things don't happen according to plan, your reset will help you bounce back faster and continue the KFG cycle.

We'll dive deeper in the upcoming sections, and I'll give you more SOS exercises to help you go.

SHIFT TO NEUTRAL

Let's return, for a few moments, to Chad's story. The hand this teenage boy was dealt was unfair and completely out of his control. The medical professionals had done everything they could. No one would have blamed Chad for being angry, terrified, or depressed—and yet he wasn't any of those things. He chose to respond to his reality in such a way that it became a beautiful gift he shared with everyone he met. Chad didn't know how many days he had left, but he chose to make the best of every one of them so he could share his gift with as many people as possible before his time was up.

All of us have a decision to make about how we choose to respond to our situations, about how we show up in the world. When we talk about responses, however, we typically only focus on the two extremes: positive and negative.

Positive responses may look something like this:

- I'm going to get this promotion!
- I'm going to ace this test!
- We are going to win this game!

Positive responses tend to be more optimistic, and this definitely is not the wrong approach, but it can sometimes veer into toxic positivity. There are moments in life where we can't lean on positivity or optimism as our default because it's false or fake. If you're in a challenging situation that requires extra strength, responding with false positivity can actually lead to self-sabotage. And quite frankly, when we are navigating the hard stuff in life, the last thing we want to hear is someone saying, "Look at the glass as half full." That can feel impossible, which leads to avoidance and a feeling of hopelessness. Sometimes we literally cannot fake it until we make it. Toxic positivity can steer you in a backward direction.

Let's say, for example, that you think, *For sure, I'm going to get this promotion and a huge bonus!* While it sounds great that you have confidence in yourself, you also could be setting yourself up for a huge disappointment that knocks you backward.

Positivity, however, is always better than negativity. Some examples of negative responses:

- I'm never going to get this promotion.
- I'm a terrible employee.
- I'm going to look foolish.
- What is everyone going to think of me?
- We're going to lose this game.

> The pause is extremely important when choosing how you want to respond. It gives you a chance to look at the facts and determine the reality of the moment.

Negativity is the most powerful response, and it's the easiest to default to because you don't have to take accountability for your life and happiness. But here's the secret: negativity always works . . . for the negative!

Now, some people live in that space, and they're okay with it. They lack the desire and ability to control their destiny. Quite frankly, they're not willing to do the work.

But that's not you. You're looking for tools, not how to take the easy way out.

So I'd like to introduce you to the space between positive and negative: neutral. Imagine it just like driving a car. Positive is drive, negative is reverse. Somewhere in between is neutral. If you try to shift straight from drive to reverse, you're going to grind your gears and badly damage your transmission. But neutral gives you a chance to pause in the middle. To allow space between something happening and your reaction to it.

To take a breath and stay still for a moment.

The pause is extremely important when choosing how you want to respond. It gives you a chance to look at the facts and determine the reality of the moment. Are you telling yourself some sort of story? If so, is it true? Is there a behavior you could change? What would that look like?

Most importantly, pausing before you respond to an event gives you time to evaluate what you need to do next. *What is your next best step?*

To go back to our earlier example of someone hoping to get a promotion, this person can't know whether they're going to get that promotion or not. To decide it is going to happen? That's called fortune-telling. But they can live in neutral, somewhere between "of course I'm going to get it!" and "there's no way I'll ever get it!" With a pause, they can evaluate what they need to do, and thus give themselves the best chance for the promotion. This person can live in the neutral response of "I'm going to be courageous and learn from this opportunity."

When I sat next to Chad on that plane, I didn't realize at the time that he was living in neutral. I was a kid; I didn't have the vocabulary for this concept. But as I learned about neutral living and the power of the pause, as I looked back and remembered his impact, I realized that he embodied it perfectly. And that brief time with him, that one flight, is where my curiosity came from, where I started to get interested in how someone could look at facts, and not tie emotion to them, dramatize them, or embrace false positivity.

Be aware, though, that you are not always going to exist perfectly in neutral. Things are going to ebb and flow, from positive to negative, as you recognize where you are and choose to shift back to neutral. The important part is to be aware of where you are, notice how you are starting to respond, and then make the shift—that is what is going to allow you to take your next best step, one from a neutral position rather than an extreme one.

For a deeper understanding of neutral I urge you to dive into the books *It Takes What It Takes* and *Getting to Neutral,* both by late author Trevor Moawad. The concept of living in neutral has been the most impactful element of support for me in my career and my life. I was introduced to these life-changing books by a client I was supporting. I will never forget the day during one of our conversations when he asked me, "Krista, have you ever heard of Trevor Moawad?" As of then, I had not, but I was very curious. He mentioned that my style of coaching that focuses on awareness, accountability, and action was quite similar to what he had read on the pages of these books. I immediately picked up a copy and dove in.

It was Easter morning 2022 when I read the last page of the book. In the final sentences, Moawad writes: "And wherever you are on your life's path, I hope that after reading this book you accept all that's happened because you also know that none of what happened in the past predicts the future. Every moment is its own adventure. . . . So you own that next moment. And the next. And the next. . . . And you keep going."[2, 3]

I closed the book, tears streaming down my face with a sense of warmth and the feeling that that book was a message. There was something greater on the horizon that had nothing to do with me, but was a calling for me. I immediately reached out to the organization that Trevor cofounded with Russell Wilson, Harry Wilson, and D.J. Eidson. It's called Limitless Minds. And I surrendered.

Months later, I received a message from D.J. We connected virtually over coffee, shared our stories (and maybe some tears), and the rest is history. Today I am grateful to support others through the power of neutral thinking as one of their speakers and workplace performance coaches. This was never part of my resume. It was never part of my dream or path. But because I leaned in with my heart, aligned with my values of joy and connection, and was able to share my story with courage and intent for the greater service of others, our paths were joined. We often say, at Limitless, "We are stronger together," and I believe there is great truth in the power of this statement.

SOS: THREE CS

I am often asked: "Once I notice I am responding in a way that does not support me, what can I do? How can I shift to neutral quickly?"

You can use a tool I call the three Cs: *catch it, control it, change it.*

Let's say that inner critic voice is playing a false narrative: "Don't screw up this meeting with a big client. Your boss will be upset and think you were a mistake taking the lead on this project. Everyone will see that you are in over your head!" No. First, *catch it.* This thought is happening right now. Next, *control it.* You are in the driver's seat, not that negative voice, and not the inner critic who's trying to take over. Finally: *change it.* Sometimes I'll say it out loud: "Nope, you're not taking control. Shut it down!"

Being aware of when this is happening is huge because it allows you to take control over those moments and hold yourself accountable for making a change, and this is how you take your next best step.

SOS: E + R = O

Although my flight sitting next to Chad was the first time I really saw how powerful this step could be, I wouldn't learn a tool to express it until years later while sitting in the audience of a leadership training session with Jack Canfield, coauthor of the *Chicken Soup for the Soul* series and *The Success Principles*. One simple formula led to a "holy cow!" moment for me and transformed the way I look at my life.

The formula: $E + R = O$. An event, plus your response to it, equals the outcome.

It may seem simple or obvious now, but at the time it was like all the lights came on and I could see everything clearly. *Oh my gosh,* I thought, *I have control over my response!*

Before that moment, I hadn't realized that I was making choices and responding in ways that were not supporting me. At that time I was on a pilgrimage with the intention of healing through the mass shooting with the goal of not letting it define me—but I had no idea what that healing looked like or how I would do it. I read every self-help book I could find and went to all the live events I could, searching for answers as I was building my business and raising my family at the same time. Really, however, I was avoiding the healing by diving full-body into all these possible solutions. In that eureka moment, though, I realized it was up to me—and only me—to make a change in my response so I could live my life differently.

If you're having the same light bulb moment I was, congratulations! You get to respond differently! You don't have to choose the same response over and over if it's not serving you. Because guess what? There will always be some unpleasant, even horrible, event that happens in your life. But *you* can determine the outcome simply based on how you respond to that event. You're in control!

As human beings, we tend to think: *I don't like this outcome. I don't like this place I'm at in my life, and it's because of the event that happened.* But that misses the whole point of where we do have control! We're here because of the way we respond to everything that happens to us. When we think an event is to blame, we're avoiding the accountability of being able to create something different.

You can't go back and change the event. It's in the past, where it's 100 percent out of your control, so there's no point in looking backward. This is what causes us to get—and remain—stuck in our story. It certainly was for me.

The only thing you have control over is the way you respond to those events in your life, which is what then gives you the outcomes you're in. So anytime you're in an outcome you don't want, it's up to you to choose to respond differently.

It can be hard to say that, to swallow it. "Krista," you may be saying, "I did not choose to get cancer." That's not what I'm saying. You're right; that's not a choice. But you can choose how you respond. And it's okay to respond with sadness; that's a very normal human response to devastating news. There may come a time when you can choose another response, when you allow sadness in but also choose joy—not one or the other, but both. And through that process of allowing both in, you can start to transition away from just feeling sadness into different responses that serve you better.

If you are guilty of blaming an event rather than focusing on your response, you're not alone! I've had conversations with leaders of large organizations, employees, parents, kids—you name it. We all think this way at some point. So recognize that you're in good company—but now get to work to change your response.

So what if you decide to respond differently? What does that look like?

How can you respond in a way that will lead to a better outcome? How can you change the way your thought patterns have formed around this event? What would that look like—and what would the possible outcomes be?

MAURICE

Maurice, a key leader in his organization, saw what this looked like after coming to me for coaching. When we first spoke, he was disappointed that he hadn't received a much-desired promotion. He told me, "I feel like I deserved that promotion, and I'm so frustrated and upset I didn't get it! I'm going to give my two weeks' notice and move my family back to the state where I grew up."

Let's break down the formula for Maurice's situation. The event was a coworker receiving the promotion he had hoped for. His response was anger, frustration, and threatening to leave the company. Had he followed through with that response, the outcome would have been to jump ship, sabotaging his career and everything he had worked so hard for. (To put it in language we learned in the first section, his inner critic was driving the car, and he was making a decision based on a false narrative.)

Again, it's easy to want to blame the event: my boss is a jerk, they don't understand, they don't support me or respect me. But, in truth, the responsibility was on *Maurice* to do the work. He didn't really want that outcome, so we worked together to change his response.

After some discussion, Maurice acknowledged that he understood why they gave the promotion to the coworker. She also was quite deserving and had been in her role a little longer than Maurice had been in his. He admitted that he adored the team he worked with and didn't want to work for anyone else.

He was happy for the coworker who got the promotion but still sad for himself, so he decided to stick it out at his company while allowing himself to take some space. He started asking, "This is an aspiration that's important to me, so how can I show up differently? How can I improve in my career?" By choosing to respond from a place of curiosity and growth, Maurice set himself up for future success. Ultimately, he got a new position within the same organization.

As Maurice learned, when you start shifting your response, you get a different outcome—guaranteed.

Maurice's example is extremely common. When we are aiming for a goal, work hard for it, feel deserving of it, and it does not happen, it can damage our ego and test us to the core. The difference stands between the person and their choice in that moment of adversity. If Maurice had listened to his inner critic and allowed it to take over, he would have displayed, in real time, the reason he may have not been ready for that particular promotion and raise. You see, when we choose to respond negatively when things do not go according to our plan, we show others that we are not resilient, not able to adapt to challenging situations. When Maurice decided to control his response from a neutral space, he became curious and asked for feedback and support to identify gaps in his skill set that would help him prepare for "what's next." His "missed opportunity" became a new opportunity based on his choice of response. It is in these moments that we are under the microscope. These moments of challenge, change, and adversity, and how we navigate them, are what can make all the difference. It takes hard work, but it is worth it!

SOS: PONO

A final tool to use to Go is PONO. *Pono* is a Hawaiian word that means being in harmony with yourself and the world. Living the *pono* life means doing the right thing—for yourself, for others, and even for the environment.

I have a deep connection to Hawaii—my husband and I got married there, my grandparents lived there, my parents have a home there now, and we still try to go back every year—so that word has always meant a lot to me. My grandmother Tutu (*tutu* is Hawaiian for grandmother) gave each of us a rock with the word *pono* on it because one of her values was doing the right thing for herself and her family. I keep that rock with me as a visual reminder to live in harmony.

Because the word *pono* was so meaningful to me, I created an acronym from it to create a moment of reflection as we take action.

P: Pause

O: Observe

N: Neutral

O: Onward

First, *pause*. Allow space in the moment to remind yourself: am I acting on the step I said was the most important one? Am I holding myself accountable? Am I moving in that direction? Am I aligned with the values I've identified?

This pause brings awareness to the surface and gives you the chance to take a breath and slow down.

Make sure not to skip this step, because without the P, *pono* just becomes "oh no!" A lot of the large, fast-paced organizations I work with push back on this, telling me, "We don't have time to pause! We have to figure out the action steps, we have to keep going, we have to hold our teams accountable!" I challenge them to make their pause extra long, because they need that pause even more. This moment of pause is what allows you to have the blank space you need to allow the truth to come out before you can align with and take action on your next best step.

Next, *observe*. Observe all of the truth in the moment. Ask questions like: am I taking action? Am I letting the inner critic take the wheel? Am I making excuses for why I can't or don't want to do this—and if so, *why*? Am I overwhelmed? Do I have too much on my plate? A sick child at home? A problem with an account at work? Am I feeling sad? Happy?

Break down the pause and observe, honestly, what's happening. You have to observe the reality of the situation to break down false narratives.

Next, we look at the situation through a *neutral* lens. Are you responding from a neutral place, neither super positive nor negative? Shift into neutral where you aren't swinging from high to low and back.

Finally, what does *onward* look like from this moment? It might not be Go yet, because something got in the way of taking your next best step. But what is something you *can* do to move onward and get closer to that action step? We have to keep moving in life, one foot in front of the other.

PONO is not just an exercise to do during a breakdown; it can apply to anything. For example, leaders of organizations can better guide their teams using PONO.

First, pause and reflect on how your team is doing right now. Is it communicating well? Are you hitting your numbers? Observe what the team members are doing to make things happen—or not happen. Are you experiencing huge sales and knocking it out of the park? Shift into neutral to figure out how to sustain that growth. Or, if things are not working as well as you'd like, shift into neutral to determine how to make a change. Determine the next best step, then take action to keep moving onward.

SOS: BREAK IT DOWN

One of the best tools for taking your next best step is to break that step down even more, into smaller, more manageable steps.

Let's say one of your goals is to get more exercise. You know where you're at: you're not as physically fit as you'd like to be, maybe you're feeling lethargic, and you know you're ready to make this change. You focus on your response: you understand that the negative self-talk—"I'm a slob; I'm so lazy"—is never going to work. You also know that toxic positivity—"I'm going to be in the best shape of my life in a month!"—is unrealistic and can set you up for failure. You must find a neutral space and determine what the next best step is. For this example, maybe it's going to the gym on a regular basis.

Great! Once you know your next best step, you're ready to take action! But wait; that big step is actually made up of many smaller steps!

The first micro-step might be something as straightforward as getting off the couch. We often focus too far ahead of where we're at, and that prevents us from taking action because we're already overwhelmed. If your goal is to get to the gym, and you're visualizing yourself on the weight machine, pumping iron, but you're still sitting on the couch at home, that's too big of a leap. So break it down into micro-steps that add up to your goal, and first visualize yourself getting off the couch. Congratulations! You've actually taken action on the first, best step toward getting yourself where you want to be!

We often focus too far ahead of where we're at, and that prevents us from taking action because we're already overwhelmed.

Once you're up, go fill your water bottle. Then change into your workout clothes. Lace up your shoes. Each of these smaller changes adds up to a big change. Before you know it, you're in your car, you've buckled your seatbelt, and you've driven to the gym, parked, and gone inside. You made it! All these micro goals were successful, and now you're at the gym ready to achieve your goal of working out.

By breaking down your next best step into bite-sized chunks, it becomes almost impossible not to take each little action. The step doesn't feel so overwhelming, which is especially important when you're starting to do something that is not part of your normal routine. And as you keep taking these smaller steps, they add up to big wins.

POOP IN THE POOL

I want to share one more example of someone who is the epitome of living in neutral, and this is a personal story because it's about my grandmother, Tutu. She was a powerhouse of a woman who advocated for treating others with respect—and she just so happened to also be hilarious and, at the same time, a woman who wouldn't take BS from anyone.

On a visit when our family was all together, my brother took his kids to the water park. They were all swimming and having a great time . . . until the lifeguards yelled for everyone to get out of the water; they were shutting down the pool for the rest of the day. You guessed it: poop in the pool.

My grandmother and I were standing in the kitchen when my brother came running in, yelling, "Poop in the pool! There's poop in the pool!"

He and his kids were so disgusted, but my grandmother just started laughing. "Isn't that just the theme of life?" she said. "Poop in the pool. Go wash it off and keep moving."

That became a common joke in our family. Anytime anything went south, we'd laugh and say, "It's just poop in the pool. Go wash it off and keep moving."

A couple of years later, Tutu was diagnosed with pancreatic cancer. Before she went in for surgery, we were in the room with her. She was all gowned up, not sure if she would make it through the surgery, and, if she did, certainly unclear of what the results would be.

She looked at us and said, "Poop in the pool. Let's go!"

She even had rocks carved for all of us that say "Poop in the pool." I like to grab that rock anytime life throws a curveball at me as a reminder to not just sit there in the midst of the shit, but to get the hell out and get myself washed off while I'm at it!

She looked at us and said, "Poop in the pool. Let's go!"

What do you need to do to clean it up? That's your next best step.

The night before my grandmother passed, my mom and I were sitting with her. She could tell her time was near, and we leaned in close to hear her. You know what she said, even though she was barely audible, her voice just a whisper?

Of course you do. You can say it with me!

"Poop in the pool."

She passed away on July seventeenth, and her funeral was on the twenty-fifth, which is the birthday for one of my daughters. We had to postpone Brooklynn's party to go to the service, but once we got home, we told her she could choose whatever she wanted to celebrate.

Being a kid with a July birthday, she wanted to go swimming. So we picked up her friends and piled into the car, excited to cool off and enjoy a day together, even if it was a couple of days after her actual birthday.

When we got to the swimming pool, however, the gate was closed. Sure enough, what did the sign say?

"Pool closed for maintenance." We all knew what that meant: poop in the pool! (We hear you, Tutu!)

How many poop-in-the-pool moments have you encountered? Remember, it's poop in the pool. Wash it off and keep going!

SURRENDER: DR. PATRICK BISHER

The second pillar of the Go step is to *surrender and reset.*

I'm going to make a slight change in the book here. I want to turn the next account over to Dr. Patrick Bisher, a former Navy SEAL, mental toughness consultant, and founder of the GRIT Academy. I want to allow Dr. Bisher, in his words, to share how he learned to surrender and to KFG.

There are levels to hitting rock bottom—one person's threshold could be another person's daily grind. I feel like I've been at the lowest of lows and highest of highs, in the most challenging and most adverse environments.

At the age of nine, I developed vascular necrosis—a rare disease that resulted in the deterioration of my left hip. I was on crutches and leg braces, like Forrest Gump, for more than a year. After experimental surgery, I was in a body cast for two months. Then, after a second surgery, I was on crutches again for another six months. That was my rock bottom as an adolescent, when I was stuck.

And that's where I was starting from—doctors told me I would never be able to walk again. But that didn't mean it was true. I wasn't going to let anyone put a limit on what I could do.

When I was younger, I had a victim's mentality—woe is me, all this bad stuff is happening to me!—but I flipped it to proving everybody wrong.

It was then that I developed what I call a 1 Percent Mentality. Doctors told me that I'd never be 100 percent, so I asked them what percentage I was at. If they said I could do 64 percent of what I used to, then that was my new 100 percent. So what could I do today to get 1 percent better than I was yesterday? To keep going—physically, emotionally, mentally, and spiritually—I kept asking, "What can I do to better myself today, just 1 percent?"

Step by step, 1 percent at a time, I was determined to get better, prove everybody wrong, and show them I could walk again. Then, if I could walk, could I get to the next step—could I run? Play sports? I didn't care if it was painful, because pain is the source of growth. I was told all these things I shouldn't do because of the pain, but if I allowed pain to dictate my future, then I would still be in a wheelchair. And was it painful? Yes. But was it necessary to get to the next step? Absolutely. Without pain, you can't have that growth. I figured out that if I could grit my teeth and grind it out, I could do anything.

I kept taking that one step at a time all the way through Basic Underwater Demolition/SEAL training, or BUD/S, which is where I encountered the famous Hell Week. Every day I was trying to earn my Trident, competing against Olympic medalists and Division I athletes. I even competed against a silver medalist on a 2-mile nautical swim. He quit; I kept fighting on [KFG – Krista, author]—not because I was a better swimmer than him, but because I mentally refused to give up. I was struggling through terrible weather conditions and mentally and physically exhausted, but I kept going.

I took all of SEAL training one evolution at a time, just like that saying: how do you eat an elephant? One bite at a time. If I looked ahead, at the seven weeks of the first phase of training, then seven more weeks, then seven more weeks after that—that's daunting. Even just Hell Week, during which you basically stay awake for an entire week, with only two two-hour naps—if I tried to take it from Sunday to Friday, I'd think: I can't do this for a week. Are you kidding me? I can't run four miles here. I can't run with a boat on my head for five miles.

But the people who had the most success took it one evolution at a time. I just wanted to get to the next meal, because I knew if I could do that, I'd get fed, I'd have more energy, and I could keep going, one foot in front of the other. Could I take the next step? Yeah. I was dealing with pain, but I just lied and said I was fine. Could I do lunges holding up a telephone pole for two and a half hours on the beach? I didn't know. But could I do just one more lunge? Maybe, yeah. Then maybe I could do another, then another, until I was done.

In the SEALs, we have the slogan "embrace the suck." The reality is that no matter what situation you're in, no matter how hard it is, you have to embrace the now, the moment you're in, so you can take that next step in the right direction.

Around me, I saw other people ring the bell, signifying that they were choosing not to go any further, but I was still there—and that let me know I had the mental fortitude to keep going as long as I could endure the pain and the process to get to the next stage.

Then one day, during training, I had a really bad static line parachute accident. I jumped out of the plane, and it was not the best of conditions. When I landed, the crosswinds meant I was going thirty miles an hour instead of fifteen; basically, like falling out of a second-story window. I hit the ground hard, heard a loud pop, and even cracked my helmet. I felt fire inside my hip socket. After feeling pain my whole life, that moment it was so intense I knew something was really wrong. But I had to keep going. I had growth and resilience—but I didn't have integrity yet, because I hadn't learned to be vulnerable enough to raise my hand and say, "Hey, something's wrong. I need help."

I kept going, but I wasn't ultimately able to perform. I dropped the guy I was carrying, and when he fell his night-vision goggles hit his nose. He was all bloody and cursing at me—rightfully so. I was humiliated because I didn't do my job.

After that injury, I had to get a hip replacement. Once again, a doctor told me something I didn't want to hear: I could no longer be a Navy SEAL. That's when I hit rock bottom professionally. I couldn't perform my duties anymore. I couldn't even put my socks on by myself; my wife had to help me. I went from humiliated to humbled.

I surrendered on that doctor's bench, telling God, "However you want to use me, use me." That surrender allowed me to move from being selfish to selfless. I was able to serve the SEAL teams, and specifically, my platoon, at a completely different level. I learned how to speak, read, and write Arabic so I could communicate with the local population where we were deployed. I was an asset instead of a liability, able to go places none of my other platoon mates went (and they went places I couldn't). I was only able to fulfill that mission because I did surrender.

God continued opening new doors for me to serve others in different capacities, and to share my testimony. In that service, I'm coaching high-level professionals. I've written books and started a mentorship program. I was able to get my doctorate of ministry and Christian leadership. It's been a blessing.

I'm not perfect, though; I screw up all the time. When you have ego come into play or let pride seep in and really punish you, you get destroyed from the inside out—holding onto that would be an issue for me. I try to put that in check every day, with integrity, by being authentic and real and letting people know I don't know it all and don't have it all.

Being a husband and father is challenging to me because they [wife and children] expect me to have these high expectations of them. I don't want my son to play sports and be a collegiate athlete; I want him to be the best version of himself that he can be. That is challenging as a leader—you have to find the gifts people have that are specific to them.

People look at me through a different lens because I was a SEAL. They think: He's the most valuable because he's the tip of the spear. Well, there's the huge, long stick behind the tip of the spear that's actually thrusting the spear forward. It's the Navy, the cook, the guy on the tarmac—every single person who's part of that team. They each have their own gift. I love being the tip of the spear. But it doesn't mean you're better than anyone else. We're all created equally. You just have to find what that gift is, and to utilize it just might take a little bit of time.

I believe God made you for a purpose. When you feel inadequate and think maybe you're not serving your purpose, it just hasn't been revealed to you. Through time, if you surrender to God, you will be able to see what that purpose is.

As Dr. Bisher shared—and as you saw in J.R.'s and Lori's stories in the first section, and in my story in the opening—there comes a moment when your next best step is to surrender. Dr. Bisher had already done all the other work. He had awareness and accountability. He was aligned with his values and living with intention. He shifted to neutral and was ready to go onward. Finally, he just surrendered.

All of us have to reach this point to have the ability to go onward.

I used to feel so much pressure and anxiety: *Is my marriage going to survive? Am I a good mom? Am I going to make an impact on others?* When I surrendered, I stopped asking those kinds of questions. None of my problems were catastrophic; my life was not ending. I was doing the best I could, in the moment of life I was in, and was able to surrender to the outcomes and allow my story to unfold.

None of my problems were catastrophic; my life was not ending. I was doing the best I could, in the moment of life I was in, and was able to surrender to the outcomes.

Surrender.

Lori used to have anxiety about losing her parents. If they weren't there to support her, how would she survive? After navigating through her grief of losing both of them, she worried about what would happen if her husband were to pass away. How could she live all alone in the world? But after our conversations, as I walked alongside Lori to help her navigate her next best steps, the world didn't feel so dark and heavy. She told me, "If the worst-case scenario actually happened, I would still be okay."

Lori surrendered to the understanding that she has all the power within herself to live a full life. She surrendered to the unknown—and though at times life could feel heavy, it wasn't so scary anymore. She had the mental strength and tools to self-navigate and thrive in a world of unknown outcomes.

J.R. surrendered to whatever came next, including firing himself from his job, having an honest conversation with his wife, and baring the secrets he'd kept hidden inside for so long.

Dr. Bisher surrendered to God and trusted in His wisdom to guide him in taking those next best steps, even if the path in front of him no longer looked as it once had.

I have a coaching client who works for a major media outlet. After working together for about three years, the other day he told me, "Krista, I'm just so burned out."

As we saw in the Know section, when someone talks about burnout, the majority of the time it means they're stuck—often because they're sabotaging their personal boundaries or sacrificing their self-care.

My client went on to say, "You know what? I need to just allow myself to surrender to the way life is unfolding and refocus on how I'm showing up as it unfolds."

As he said that—and he did so with no prompting from me—I thought: *That's it!*

That is the last action step of the KFG process: surrender. Surrender control of how life unfolds. Lean into the way you show up. We feel like we don't have time to surrender in the moment, to take a pause for personal boundaries or self-care, but we can't afford *not* to.

Surrendering doesn't mean you're giving up, throwing in the towel, or waving the white flag. It means going all-in on yourself. In fact, surrendering is the opposite of giving up. It means you're done being at war with yourself. You're done running on a hamster wheel. It means letting go of the control you don't have and loving yourself enough to show up *for yourself* as life unfolds as it's going to.

Surrender so you can simply keep going.

SOS: FORGIVE YOURSELF TO LOVE YOURSELF

As you navigate through the KFG Formula, and through the major sections of this book, you're learning how to forgive yourself. As humans, we strive for perfection, but perfection is a myth. With KFG, you're always striving for improvement with the understanding that perfection is not the goal because it is impossible to achieve.

In order to KFG, you have to forgive yourself. And you are going to have to forgive yourself over and over again. That is how you get to the place of deep self-love.

You may not be able to forgive yourself 100 percent—you don't have to fully forgive yourself for every mistake and misstep—but know that you, we, all of us, are continually a work in progress. We're always having breakdowns within ourselves. We KFG and have another breakdown—and then we KFG again. When you make a mistake, be honest about it. Have the courage to be open, transparent, and vulnerable. Then forgive yourself and KFG.

Eventually, you'll realize that you don't have to forgive yourself daily; you'll just understand that you're not supposed to be perfect. You can't be perfect. Part of that self-love is embracing your imperfections and moving forward anyway. And you can't move forward until you forgive yourself.

In the beginning of my breakdown after Las Vegas, I was so stuck in blame-and-complain, in trying to make the world the villain in my story. Once I forgave myself, I realized how much time I wasted in that space—and I forgave myself for that, too.

You may be wondering: How do I do this? How do I forgive myself? Answer: by using the KFG Formula you've learned here. As you KFG, you're showing up differently, working on yourself, trying to improve this one life you have. In making those improvements, you're giving yourself the best gift: love. You love yourself enough to make a change. Don't you love yourself enough to let go of the past as well? If you truly, deeply love yourself, why would you not forgive yourself?

I remember telling myself, "I just want to get back to how it used to be." But again, that's impossible. Things can never be like they were, because we can never re-enter the past. Would you really want to go backward anyway? In the cold of winter you may think, "I can't wait for summer!" And summer will happen again, but it's not going to be exactly the same as last summer. That's life. It changes, and it's never the same, and you can try to wish it away all you want, but that's a waste of time and energy.

At some point you experience a moment where you mourn the idea of who you thought you were going to be . . . and then start embracing the person you're becoming. Give yourself the gift of growth and accept that you are exactly where you're supposed to be—and exactly who you're meant to be—to meet this moment. Forgive yourself for the idea that you're supposed to be someone you're not.

You're not done becoming who you're supposed to be. You have possibilities, opportunities, growth ahead of you. And you'll never be done. Every time you get to the G, you'll start again with another K, the next F, a different G. You'll never get to the point where you look for the next best step only to find nothing—not until your final breath on earth.

Forgive who you were, accept who you are, and love all of yourself—including the person you are becoming. You're worth it!

FOCUS ON THE JOURNEY, NOT THE DESTINATION

As you are figuring out your next best step, one of the most important pieces of advice I can give is to focus on the journey, not the destination. Focus on *this* moment, right now, not the ones you envision to come.

This can be incredibly difficult, especially if you're a high achiever with big ambitions, dreams, and goals. You just want to get there! You want it to happen *now*. And in this world of instant gratification, we've all become accustomed to having the world at our fingertips. We're guaranteed a response to text messages and social media posts and emails, and all in about twelve seconds.

How often do we all get caught up in the destination? I can't count how many times I've driven from home to work or to my kids' school and I'll get to the parking lot before I realize I don't remember any of the drive. I was just on autopilot!

> When I catch myself driving on autopilot, I like to try taking a different route. All of a sudden you start seeing new sights, and you gain an appreciation for the interesting things that were there all along—if only you'd stopped to look.

For your life's journey, you have to slow down and focus on the moment in front of you now, because that is the only moment that matters. The moment you are in *right now* is the stepping-stone for the next moment you want to get to—and the next, then the next, then the next after that.

I coached Jose for a year and a half before he was able to absorb this lesson. He came to me because he wanted to become more aware of how he was showing up and looking at his career. He was thirsty to grow. In fact, he used the words, "I want a seat at the executive table."

But he was so focused on the end result that he wasn't looking at the actions in his current moments to see what would get him there.

One day he told me about stopping at a coffee shop on his way to work. There were two people ahead of him in line having a conversation with the barista. "Krista," he told me, "I was *so annoyed.* I wanted to just say, 'Can you just hurry up and get your damn coffee and get out of my way!?' I had so much to do."

> He began to realize he was envious of the people in the conversation. They were calm, relaxed, and enjoying each other's company.

He continued. "Then I realized that I don't want to respond like this. I want to be cool."

He began to realize he was envious of the people in the conversation. They were calm, relaxed, and enjoying each other's company. Maybe the end result he thought he wanted was not allowing him to enjoy his here-and-now. Maybe he cared more about peace and fulfillment.

When he reached work, he realized that what he was looking for in life . . . was exactly what those two coffee shop customers had. They were so happy in the moment; they didn't care what was going on around them or what they'd be doing in an hour! Meanwhile, Jose had finished the coffee he'd purchased, but he didn't even remember tasting it because he was so focused on getting to his next meeting.

I understand where Jose was coming from, and I'm guessing you do too. We all want to be the best version of ourselves, and when we're constantly evaluating what that looks like and how the hell we can get there, it adds extra stress and pressure to our lives.

Living in pause, in the current moment, doesn't take any extra time or effort. It just takes a little refocusing. Life is made up of the little moments. Focus on them, and you will see that life is a beautiful journey.

WHAT'S GETTING IN YOUR WAY? (SPOILER: IT'S YOU!)

You may be surprised to know how many individuals I've spoken with who know exactly what it takes to become elite, to be their best selves, and who have done the hard work of the K and the F—but then get stuck because they don't take action.

What's getting in their way? What's getting in your way and keeping you from taking action? Well, spoiler alert, it may just be *you*. It's not the weather, it's not being sick, it's not somebody else—it's you. It's always you.

After all the hard work you've done this far, you're so close to taking that next best step that you can taste it—but you're stuck and getting in your own way.

Maybe you are still battling a fear of failure. When we're on the cusp of taking action to make a big change, our old habits and tendencies pop up because habits are hard to break—and one of the hardest habits is likely the one that got us into this situation to begin with. Self-sabotage leads to getting stuck and allowing ourselves to remain stuck.

By working the KFG Formula, you have the ability to shift and change, regardless of your situation, to take action and avoid staying stuck any longer.

Now allow me to shift to a slightly different angle. Sometimes we get stuck because we're not really ready to KFG—and that's okay. Maybe, in your heart of hearts, you're not quite ready to move forward yet. You know what it's going to take to move forward, but you're not ready to take that action yet.

If you know what it's going to take to KFG, but you are not actively leaning into it, you probably aren't yet ready to take that step. And, let's be honest, that's what separates average from elite. Now, when I say average, I want you to know that living an average life is completely fine. You can live a joyful, beautiful, happy life through average. But if you have the desire to move into being elite (and let's face it, you likely do if you're reading this book), it takes a lot of courage. A lot of vulnerability. But you can do it. When you are ready, you can lean in and let go of everything in the past, all those bad habits, and take that next best step.

If you find you're not quite ready, guess what? You get to work the KFG Formula again. *K, F, G.* Know where you're at right now. You got so damn close, so now what do you do?

You don't have to succeed on your first try. If you continue actively working the formula, it will get you closer and closer to where you want to be. If you're not ready to become that person, how can you become someone who is at least closer to where you want to be while still being comfortable with who you are? Those building blocks will help you move forward, even if that next best step isn't completely within reach yet.

This process is easy, but complex, at the same time, because it requires so much hard work and self-accountability. It takes time and patience. You don't come up with the vision of the elite person you want to become and then magically have it happen. Going through KFG is like working a puzzle. The first time you navigate it, you're going to have a couple pieces that fit but a whole bunch of pieces on the side of the table for which you have no idea where they go. But look at what you've done, at the pieces you have fit together! Each time you KFG, you'll find more and more pieces that fit together until, eventually, the entire picture becomes clear.

But maybe that's not what's holding you back. Maybe you're not scared of failure, and you're ready to get started, but you're afraid of what happens *if you actually succeed!* What if you actually take this next step, knowing it's the best one for you right now . . . and then you don't know what to do after that? The path is never clear, so taking your next best step means that eventually you're going to have to take another step, and that's scary.

But maybe that's not what's holding you back. Maybe you're not scared of failure, and you're ready to get started, but you're afraid of what happens *if you actually succeed!*

You take one step, climb one mountain—and then what? What's the *next* mountain to climb? Professional athletes turned champions frequently experience this after winning the championship game. All season long they work through the KFG, and they know exactly what it takes to win. They stay focused, stay in neutral, and keep looking for their next best step—and they freaking do it! They win!

But then they have that same "now what?" moment. Because now that they've climbed one mountain, the next one is bigger and the expectations are higher. They've just had a breakthrough—but the breakthrough creates another breakdown.

This isn't just true for athletes. Employees see it when they get a big promotion, parents see it when they look into their newborn's eyes. We all have that moment where we think, *Oh my gosh, my/our dream just came true! Holy sh*t . . . now what??*

Well, I can tell you now what: you work the KFG Formula again, because you've got a brand-new mountain to climb. Most people, however, typically don't see it like that. We don't see that it's a continuous cycle, that we literally have to *keep freaking going.* It is time to reset and KFG again. When you're at the top, dust yourself off, put on a new pair of shoes, and start climbing again—because you're actually at the base of your next mountain, and you have to figure out where to go from here.

It all comes back to KFG. As my friend Josh Lifrak says, "Life doesn't get easier. We get better."

WHERE DO I GO NEXT? HOW PHIL WORKED THE KFG

Phil came to me eighteen months ago while starting a brand-new chapter of his life and feeling insecure about it. His children were grown, with his youngest son just having graduated high school and moved out of the house. Phil was suddenly an empty nester.

"Everyone talks about this moment," he told me. "But I'm just in a funk about it. I feel terrible. I miss how my life was—being needed as a father. Now I just feel kinda worthless, like I don't even know who I am if I'm not Dad, the caretaker and supporter of my family. I don't feel fulfilled in my career, and I miss my kids."

So we started working the KFG Formula. Phil was able to tell me, honestly and transparently, where he was, but he needed to hear that it was okay to feel sad, to grieve who he used to be. As he allowed that process to take place, he became even more aware of where he was in that moment—and he actually started to embrace it instead of trying to shove it away. He allowed himself to feel sad, to miss his kids, to remember how they were at two and twelve and even twenty-two.

But he didn't want to be stuck in that sadness. He didn't want to just sit there—which is so easy to do—so he looked at how he could support himself. He stepped into being accountable for his happiness. Part of that involved Phil exploring how to strengthen his relationships at work and investigating whether he actually wanted a different career or if he was looking at his friends' relationships with their work and playing the comparison game.

From there we worked to help Phil identify his values. He told me, "I really enjoy connecting with others, but I feel very lonely right now."

With the idea of connection in mind, Phil reached out and had conversations with his team members and his supervisor about their different areas of interest. We discussed more effective ways of communicating. He also set the intention of embracing his vulnerability. Phil was extremely confident in his work with numbers and data. He's smart as a whip and a high performer, but he was very guarded with his emotions and had a hard time opening up.

"It's my fiftieth birthday," he told me. "And I want to celebrate, but no one in the office even knows."

"If your intention is to be more vulnerable with your team," I said, "and you've been feeling lonely and isolated, and you want to celebrate with them, then what can you do?"

Phil decided to bring a cake to the office and invite his team to celebrate his birthday with him. And they did, rallying around him and showering him with support and affection. He began to reap the benefits of these baby steps of vulnerability, so then he was ready to focus on staying in neutral, not letting his emotions take the wheel or acting through sadness. He was able to do so by anchoring back to his value of connection and remaining accountable for his own happiness.

I spoke to Phil recently, and he said, "Krista, I'm coming to you today because you've been with me for eighteen months, and through our conversations and everything we've worked on, I want to tell you first that I have officially retired the version of who I was and have surrendered to trying to become this new version. I feel like a brand-new individual, and I'm so happy and fulfilled. Other people have even noticed the shift in me, and my wife said, 'Whatever you've been doing, keep doing it!' I just had to forgive myself for that past version and let go of where I was—trying to be the perfect husband, father, and coworker."

Phil continued talking with such gratitude, and then he asked me the question that so many people I've worked ask at this point: "Where do I go from here? I don't want to lose this—I'm so grateful and happy in this moment. What do I do next?"

"Well," I asked, "what would you say in this moment? What's your action step?"

"I'm just going to enjoy it!"

"Boom," I said. "That's exactly it. We're all striving to feel the way you feel right now. So why look for your next action step? If you're feeling it right now, what would happen if you just sat with it and enjoyed it?"

* * * * *

You might read Phil's story and think: Well, kudos to Phil—everything worked out well for him! But Phil is still navigating breakdowns—he and his son are having problems around financial responsibility. However, Phil has been through the KFG formula fully for himself, so he is aware, accountable, aligned with his values, living with intention, operating from a neutral place, and able to surrender to the results. He is able to recognize that he guided his son as far as he could, but it's his son's life. His son is going to have to make his own choices, and he may struggle and fall flat on his face as so many of us do. Phil will always be his father, and he'll do his best to support his son—but he can't control the chapters in a life book that is not his to write.

Life is never perfect, even when it's really good. But when you have all these different tools in your toolbox, you can access them and keep working with them in all the many different situations. And when you're feeling those moments of calm and peaceful flow, well . . . enjoy them. They required awareness, accountability, and proper action. You've earned it.

Before you complete this chapter, ask yourself:

- Are you aware of how far you've come?
- Have you surrendered to your old self, and do you allow your new self to be loved fully?
- Are you ready to KFG again? Then . . . *let's go!!!*

THE TWO PILLARS: SHIFT TO NEUTRAL AND SURRENDER

Use Your SOS (Strategies of Success) Tools:

- 3 Cs
- E + R = O
- PONO
- Break It Down
- Forgive Yourself to Love Yourself

Key Points to Re-evaluate

- Focus on the Journey, Not the Destination
- What's Getting in Your Way? It Could Be . . . You
- Where Do I Go Next?

Three Questions Before Moving On

- Are you aware of how far you've come?
- Have you surrendered to your old self, and do you allow your new self to be loved fully?
- Are you ready to KFG again? Then . . . *let's go!!!*

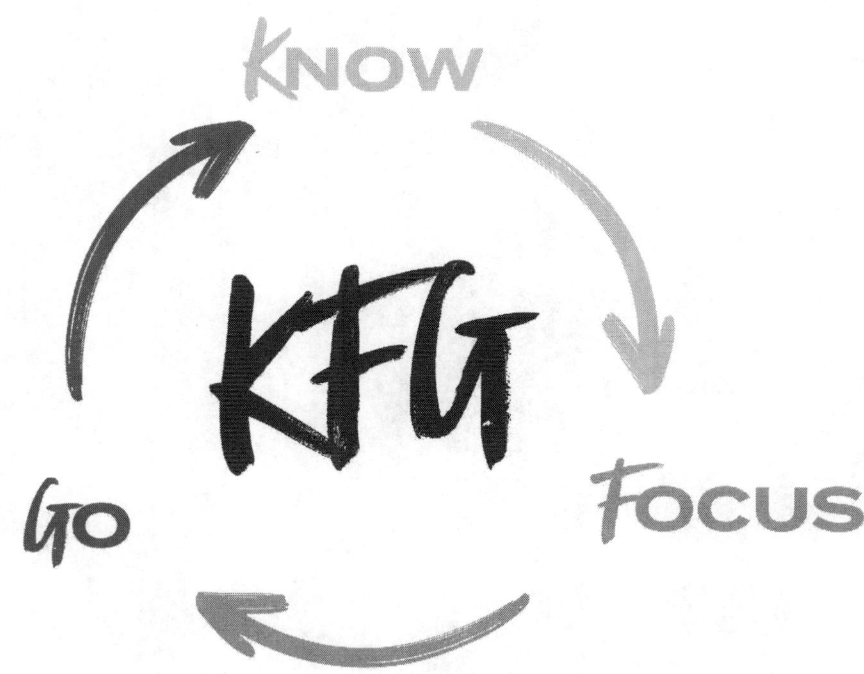
Know
KFG
Focus
Go

KFG: THE CONCLUSION (FOR NOW)

Never in my freaking life did I ever want to write a book.

When I was in Las Vegas, running from that shooter, thinking *keep fucking going* as hard as I could, I set an intention, that night, without even realizing it, without knowing what the end result would be. My intention was that if I was able to get out of that horrible event and not just survive but thrive in my life, I was going to do it in a different way. I was dedicating my journey to flipping the narrative and creating the opposite of what that person (whose name I have intentionally not used in this book) set out to do: to create chaos and destroy as many lives as possible.

It ignited a fire under me to affect as many lives as possible in a positive way, through this neutral mindset, through the KFG Formula, through helping people do the deep work of stepping into their own lives in a more supportive, loving way. That shooter's intention was such an evil one, but I feel peace and gratitude that we are able to flip moments like those and do something really powerful for the greater good.

As part of that, I knew I had to put my story out there, even if I didn't want to. Always more comfortable talking than writing, I began speaking about that night and my journey of healing afterward.

Every time I talked about it—whether in coaching, training, or as a keynote speaker—people would say, "Krista, it's like you were talking directly to me. I feel like you were telling my story."

But those stories were all completely different! I heard it from a male breast cancer survivor, from someone who lost a child to cancer, from someone navigating their third divorce—people from all different walks of life. Even though all our stories are unique, we are more similar than different.

Everyone is navigating their own KFG at a different level.

Organizations that are growing into multi-billion-dollar companies while looking to keep their foot on the gas are busy working the KFG formula. Athletes, musicians, teachers, and teenagers are busy working the KFG. Keep going, keep going, keep going.

All those people had something else in common, too: they all asked for something they could take with them. They had heard me speak about the tools to put in their toolbox, but they wanted something they could carry and look back at and remind themselves. That's why I ended up writing a book—not only because I truly believe my message is important and can help people step into their own lives and provide a better way to be more supportive for themselves and others, but also because a book is something you can hold. You can feel it, or listen to it. When you need a parachute, it's there. If you feel like you're drowning, it's something to grab onto for dear life. You can come back to it any time you need.

Talk about surrendering.

I never wanted to write a book, but I felt this absolute desire to do so because I want to encourage others to live as the best version of themselves—and the only way I can do that is by sharing and being vulnerable with who I am and what I've learned.

That is my why—the reason I wrote this book and choose to share my story with you. But truly, this has never, ever been about me. It's so much deeper than that. It's always about the *we*.

Why are we doing this? Why is this so important? What's the overarching reason for all of this? Why are we making sure we are our best selves? Why are we doing the hard work for ourselves?

Because it's not about me, or you, or any *one*; it's about all of us. It's about becoming a greater version of ourselves so we can impact the world in a better way.

Even though the KFG Formula entails a lot of internal, deep work, at the end of the process the reality comes to the surface that it's never been about one person—it's about how to improve yourself so you can show up and support others, because that is the secret sauce of life. The whole purpose of us being on this earth is so we can be our best selves. That's our accountability piece—and yet it doesn't end there. It's so we can be our best selves *in service of others.*

BONUS S.O.S.: REMEMBER YOUR WHY

A powerful way to actually take your next best step is to remember your why and tie the action back to your intention. Why are you doing this? Why is it your next best step? Why is this moment so important to you?

Tying this step to your why attaches it to the values you've carved out. It reaffirms the importance of making this change by considering the potential impact it could make while also acknowledging all the work you've done in the K, F, and G steps.

A powerful way to actually take your next best step is to remember your why and tie the action back to your intention. Why are you doing this?

Anchoring to your why is like giving yourself a pep talk as you're taking action. That can shut down any of that Mean Girl voice that tries to seep through. What if she pops up to say, "Going to the gym is stupid. Wouldn't you rather just eat some chips, drink some wine, and binge-watch that show you love?" Then you're ready to tell her, "No, I'm trying to live a healthier lifestyle so I can be here for my children and grandchildren." Or, "I want to feel better in my body." Or, "I want to be able to go skiing with my family."

All those reasons are your why—and once you start declaring your reasons why and giving yourself that pep talk, your authentic self is going to be louder than your inner critic, which means that's the one you're going to pay attention to.

A great way to truly remember your why is to find a visual reminder—something important to you, like a meaningful piece of jewelry or a picture of your family—anything that—and when you hold it or look at it, will remind you exactly why this is such an important step for you to take. We all get stuck in the day-to-day grind, where it's easy to forget to keep taking the steps we need to take, to step into that elite person we want to become. A visual reminder helps slow you down and brings awareness back to the surface. Are you actively moving on what you've defined as the next best step?

You have all the tools to make your journey a success—no matter what you're navigating.

ONE FOOT IN FRONT OF THE OTHER: THE RESET

When you've reached the end of the KFG Formula, that actually means you're back at the beginning. It starts over. Because guess what? Now you're at a different spot in your life, so you have to intentionally take the time to know where you are. You need to ask again: where do you want to go? What do you need to do to get there? How can you respond most effectively? Who's going to be there to cheer you on?

The process keeps going. It's a ball that just keeps rolling. *Keep f-ing going.* Work the process again.

KFG is cyclical in nature, and there are smaller cycles within the large cycles. If you're navigating a huge crisis or breakdown, you can do a deeper dive, but those smaller cycles are just as important because that's exactly how you move one foot in front of the other every single day.

I'm the one who created this process and wrote this book—and I need KFG as much as anyone. I have to be actively working these steps, just like you do. I will never be a KFG expert, because none of us are.

> When I wake up every day, I think, "I'm a beginner today."

One of the biggest takeaways, for me, of this entire journey is that I am going to start over as well, back at the K: *knowing* where I'm at now and where I want to go from here. When I wake up every day, I think, "I'm a beginner today." Even on that smaller scale of my daily life, I can ask, "Where am I today? What do I want to focus on? How is today going to go? What do I need to do to make the biggest impact in my day today?"

You can KFG every single day, and it starts with simply declaring yourself to be a beginner. Then the day is gone, and guess what? You KFG the next day, and the one after that.

KFG. Keep f-ing going. You got this!

SHYANNE

Shyanne is a dear friend of mine. When I met her she was in active kidney failure and on an extremely long wait-list for a donor kidney. There were so many people ahead of her for a transplant, and her doctors told her that she needed a new kidney soon. Due to all this, she realized, "If I don't do something, I am going to die."

But she made a courageous choice: she shifted to neutral. She wasn't telling herself, "I'm going to get through this, I'm going to survive." That would have been toxic positivity, because there were no guarantees. If she didn't get a transplant, she wouldn't survive—those were the facts. But she didn't swing into negativity either. She did not want to think, *That's it. I'm going to die. There's nothing I can do, it's not going to happen, my life is over.*

Shyanne swallowed down all her feelings of fear, guilt, and shame. She had T-shirts printed and signs made for her car that said, "I need a kidney. Can you help save my life?"

She told me, "Do you know how embarrassing it was to drive around, begging people to acknowledge that maybe they could save my life?" She was an important leader in an organization, and she felt like she had to set all her pride aside, become vulnerable, and beg people to notice her. But she chose to respond in this way because she wanted to live. That was her next best step, the best chance she had to live. She could hold onto her pride and face the possibility of dying . . . or get over her embarrassment and shame and take the courageous action of putting it out into the universe, of saying, "I need help."

Eight individuals stepped up and reached out to Shyanne because of those signs. Unfortunately, none of them were matches—but Shyanne realized she wasn't alone. There were beautiful people out there who wanted to help.

> It never would have happened if she hadn't taken that step and shared her story, if she hadn't become vulnerable enough to ask for help.

One night she was at a friend's house; they were chatting and canning salsa together. As they were talking, her friend's stepdaughter entered the room and asked, "Hey, what are you guys talking about?"

Shyanne said, "I was just saying how I need a kidney transplant, but I haven't been able to find a match yet."

The stepdaughter, a math teacher, said, "Well, this is a simple math problem: I have two kidneys, you need one. You can have one of mine."

She went through the testing, and the young woman ended up being such a close match that the lab thought they were related.

In 2019, both women underwent surgery. Shyanne received the kidney transplant that saved her life. But it never would have happened if she hadn't taken that step and shared her story, if she hadn't become vulnerable enough to ask for help—and accept the gift someone was able to give her.

Shyanne had to push like heck through all her fear and become extremely vulnerable. It was literally a matter of life and death—she had to set aside all her pride and fear and do everything in her power to advocate to save her own life. Shyanne is the epitome of KFG!

To share your KFG story, please visit
www.myKFGstory.com.

WE'RE ALL IN THIS TOGETHER

The night of the shooting, I was alone. I got separated from everyone I knew and was literally running for my life. I *thought* I was completely on my own.

In reality, I wasn't. I had so many people helping me—that night, and every day since. There are so many people in this world who are here to help. We just have to keep our eyes open so we can recognize them when we see them. And when someone helps us, we can repay them by going on to help someone else. That is how we make sure that none of us are ever navigating life in silence.

We are not alone, because we are all navigating through these experiences, even if they're not exactly the same. We're connected through our humanity. Through the commonality of letting go of who you thought you were and stepping into becoming the person you are becoming.

What can you share with someone so they know they aren't alone? What can you pour into their bucket while also filling your own? I challenge you to hold the door open for someone and not walk away feeling just a little bit better. (Try it.) Even if you don't know that person at all—even if they don't acknowledge you—that little moment matters because it connects you to another person.

As I reflect back to where I was years ago and where I am now, I'm filled with gratitude. I'm grateful I was placed within the chaos the night of October 1, 2017. Not because of the horrific events from that night and its tragic loss, but because I was shook alive.

I'm living a different life than I otherwise would have been. I was comfortable and coasting before, and now I'm living through intention. I know the life I want to live and the impact I want to make on others. It was a promise I made while running for my life that night. If I was gifted another chance, to love and live better, I would do whatever I could in my power to fulfill that promise.

The shooter who caused the mass chaos that night tried to ruin as many lives as possible. But with hard work and stepping into the best version of myself possible, I am committed to ensuring that his intentions for that night are not fulfilled. With the KFG formula, we can all live our best life and love harder than ever before.

Love always wins.

Never in my wildest dreams did I think my mantra for survival would turn into an action step for life. And guess what? It's not mine—it's all of ours. We all need to KFG and help others do the same.

You are not alone.

You are not done.

Keep f!#ing going.*

SHARE YOUR KFG STORY!

Several years ago I had a client reach out to me and say, "Krista, I've been trying to get ahold of you, but when calling, your audio message says your mailbox is full." Upon investigation I found that I had a number of old and missed voice messages yet to be deleted. Most of us have fallen victim to the overloaded inbox at some point.

For me, this was the first and last time I let my voice messages go unnoticed! As I was going through them, three of them took my breath away, stopping me in my tracks. You see, I was still contemplating writing this book. I was not sure I wanted to share my KFG story or my voice.

What might others think of it? Would it even be useful for anyone else to learn the steps that supported me? Then, like so many times in our lives, the universe gave me my answer, through this series of old voice messages that I still hold sacred on my phone today.

The first voice message was from my grandmother Tutu. She left it nine days before she passed away. "It's Grandma. Give me a quick call when you get a chance. I just wanted to hear your voice."

The second message was from my husband, Chris. It was his desperate and scared voice calling the night of the Las Vegas mass shooting. We were still separated and had not yet found each other, so he was unaware if I was safe—and had no idea where I was. "Krista, pick up your damn phone," he said. "I just want to hear your voice." The sirens and chaos sound through the background of his message.

The last message was from my dear friend Shyanne. She was reaching out to share her love and support for me knowing the challenges I was facing and the work I was doing attempting to create a new reality in my life. Her message started: "Hello, Krista. I just wanted to hear your voice . . . "

It was that day in which I committed to writing this book and bringing this formula to others and sharing my voice. You see, we are all going through KFG in our lives. Every single one of us has a story. Though our stories differ, we are all connected through our experiences.

Once we start to share these stories, we find we are more alike than different. We were *never* meant to do this thing called life alone. We are stronger together and can continue impacting others through our stories.

Do you have a KFG story? There is so much power and freedom in sharing stories! You will find out we are more alike than different.

Please share your story with me at www.myKFGstory.com.

Let me hear your voice!

REFLECTION AND ACTION

Now that you have experienced the power of the KFG formula, you are actually at the beginning. You have the choice to KFG every day.

These questions will support you in continuing the KFG journey. You will find value in reviewing these questions within your team or organization, or on an individual basis, to keep momentum going and put action behind this new way of living and leading.

Knowledge plus action equals results!

KFG FOR ORGANIZATIONS AND INDIVIDUALS NAVIGATING SUCCESS:

1. What is our (my) current state related to success?
2. What habits and behaviors supported this success?
3. How can we (I) build off this momentum?
4. What is getting in our (my) way?
5. What can I do to contribute and hold myself accountable? What does this action look like?
6. What are my top two values?
7. How am I acting through these values in alignment with my organization's values?

8. How am I setting intentions throughout the day to support success?
9. How am I choosing to respond in neutral?
10. How am I prepared to reset when things don't go according to plan? What does my reset look like?
11. How am I living in gratitude and staying focused on the blessings in this moment?
12. What is my best action step TODAY?

KFG FOR ORGANIZATIONS AND INDIVIDUALS NAVIGATING A CHALLENGE OR CHANGE:

1. What is our (my) current state related to a challenge or change?
2. How are we (I) acknowledging that our (my) past experience does not define our future success?
3. What is getting in our (my) way?
4. What are habits or behaviors that we (I) can eliminate to support our success?
5. What can I do to contribute and hold myself accountable? What does this action look like?
6. What are my top two values?
7. How am I acting through these values in alignment with my organization's values?
8. How am I setting daily intentions for growth and improvement?
9. How am I choosing to respond in neutral as I take forward action?
10. How am I prepared to reset quickly when things don't go according to plan? What does my reset look like?

11. How am I living in gratitude for the lessons of the past while staying focused on the moment and all the blessings I now have?
12. What is my best action step TODAY?

KFG QUESTIONS FOR INDIVIDUALS AND BOOK CLUBS

These questions will support you in continuing your KFG journey. You will find value in reviewing these questions on an individual basis, or with your friends and loved ones, to keep momentum going. They will also help you put action behind this new way of living.

1. What is the current reality of my life?
2. What can I do to enhance my life and hold myself accountable?
3. What does this action look like?
4. What are habits or behaviors I can eliminate to support my success?
5. What are my top two values?
6. How am I acting through these values?
7. How am I setting intentions throughout the day?
8. How am I responding in neutral?
9. How am I planning to reset when things don't go according to plan?
10. What does my reset look like?
11. How am I staying focused on the present moment and acknowledging my blessings?
12. Who will I reach out to for support and accountability?
13. What is my best action step TODAY?

RESOURCES TO SUPPORT YOUR SUCCESS

ORGANIZATIONS

Limitless Minds is the mindset and performance training solution for the modern-day corporate professional. The organization trains people in the power of neutral thinking to unlock unprecedented performance and resilience. At the heart of its philosophy lies the belief that mindset is the key to overcoming obstacles and achieving greatness. Limitless Minds offers tailored coaching, training programs, cutting-edge technological resources, and a supportive community to guide your journey. To explore how Limitless Minds can help you harness your full potential and turn challenges into stepping stones, visit https://limitlessminds.com/.

Newfield Network is an ICF (International Coaching Federation) accredited coaching program that provides training to leaders and coaches who aim to change the world. One key differentiator of the Newfield Coach training program is that it is grounded in the framework of ontology, which is the study of "being." To find out more about Newfield Network or to find a coach to support you, visit https://newfieldnetwork.com/.

The National Speakers Association (NSA) has helped tens of thousands of speakers through professional development and unparalleled community. There are NSA local chapters throughout the United States where you can connect and learn with speakers in your area. To find one near you, visit https://nsaspeaker.org/.

ImpactEleven is a speaker training, development, and accelerator community working tirelessly to develop and serve thousands of voices with infinite influence to transform lives and the world for the better. This organization is dedicated to giving thought leaders and experts unparalleled access to the people, relationships, knowledge, coaching, and skills that compress the time needed to become a better speaker with greater impact and commercial success. To find out more, visit https://impacteleven.com/.

BOOKS

Moawad, Trevor, *It Takes What It Takes: How to Think Neutrally and Gain Control of Your Life,* HarperCollins Publishers, 2020

Moawad's motivational approach is elegant but refreshingly simple: he replaces hardwired negativity, the kind of defeatist mindset that's nearly everybody's default, with what he calls "neutral thinking." His own special innovation, this is a nonjudgmental, nonreactive way of coolly assessing problems and analyzing crises, a mode of attack that offers luminous clarity and supreme calm in the critical moments before taking decisive action.

Moawad, Trevor, *Getting to Neutral: How to Conquer Negativity and Thrive in a Chaotic World,* HarperCollins Publishers, 2022

It's easy to be positive when everything is coming up roses. What happens when life goes sideways? Many of us lapse into a self-defeating negative spiral that makes it hard to accomplish anything. Getting to

Neutral is a step-by-step guide that shows readers how to use mental conditioning coach Moawad's innovative motivational system to defeat negativity and thrive.

Brothers, Chalmers and Kumar, Vinay, *Language and the Pursuit of Leadership Excellence: How Extraordinary Leaders Build Relationships, Shape Culture, and Drive Breakthrough Results,* New Possibilities Press, Inc., 2015

Language and the Pursuit of Leadership Excellence provides a framework for dramatically improving the three competencies that matter most to successful leaders:

- Conversational competencies
- Relational competencies
- Emotional competencies

It is these, far more than technical or functional competencies, that enable extraordinary leaders to do what they do—and be who they are.

Full of practical takeaways, parallels from other best-selling business authors, and real-world application, this book is essential for leaders seeking to significantly improve bottom-line results—however they are measured.

SERVICES

KFG Coaching, founded by Krista Ryan, is a business coaching company designed to support employees of organizations through confidential coaching conversations, strategy building, workplace performance, and action plans. To find out more about professional coaching, visit https://kfgcoaching.com/.

Croft Edwards, Master Certified Coach (MCC), and his organization, CROFT + COMPANY, have been helping leaders and organizations find their LeadershipFlow through coaching and leadership development since 2001. To find your #LeadershipFlow, contact Croft at https://www.croftandcompany.com/.

END NOTES

1. Orbe-Austin, Lisa, and Orbe-Austin, Richard, *Own Your Greatness* (Ulysses Press, 2020), p. 61.

2. Moawad, Trevor, *It Takes What It Takes* (HarperCollins Publishers, 2020), p. 23.

3. Moawad, Trevor, *Getting to Neutral* (HarperCollins Publishers, 2022), p. 230.

ACKNOWLEDGMENTS

To those friends, clients, and partners who contributed stories and experiences and shared your KFG moments to make this book possible: thank you! I wrote this book to reach as many individuals as possible to learn to KFG, and I could not have done it without you.

My husband, Chris. You have been by my side, through ups and downs, twists and turns. Thank you for bringing such joy to our family and life. This book would never have happened without your support and encouragement to never give up (even after my first publisher went bankrupt and I lost everything . . . KFG)! I am beyond blessed to have you in my life as my partner and best friend. Thank you for being you.

For my kids: Mason, Brooklynn, and Grace. You mean more to me than anything in the world. I am so grateful for the amazing experiences we share, the life we live, and the love you all have given me. My greatest accomplishment in life is being your mom. Not one day goes by that I don't look at you and feel like God somehow messed up and gave me three best friends instead of "kids." I feel like the luckiest person alive because of you. I can't wait to see you KFG in your own lives as you make a huge impact in this world!

For my own parents. Thank you for teaching the invaluable lessons of love, forgiveness, strength, and that family really is the most important thing in life. Dad, for teaching me to take every single shot because a few of them will "drop" and go in, and those could be the ones that make a difference! Mom, for teaching me strength and unwavering love for others. No matter what. Love always wins. This was instilled in my heart at a very early age, and I carry it with me today. Love always wins.

To the 58 angels who lost their lives the night of October 1, 2017. I will honor you and your families and continue to fight against evil by using the weapon of love for the rest of my life. For my Route 91 family. I love you. Keep F---ing Going.

For my coach, Croft Edwards, who has been with me since 2016, through some of the most challenging life moments, who has never been afraid to call me out on my BS and help me become a better speaker and coach, and to never settle and never give up. I would not be where I am today without your support.

To my Limitless Minds squad. Thank you for your trust, friendship, love, and laughter. Sharing the stage with you and supporting our clients are some of my favorite moments in life. We are better together. The best is yet to come!

To my National Speakers Association family. Before partnering with you I was unaware of the powerhouse squad of like-minded speakers and amazing humans. I am so grateful for your friendship and support. My career as a professional speaker could feel lonely at times. Then I found you and everything changed. I now have lifelong friends who cheer loud and proud for me, and who share tools, encouragement, and success with me. My career has been forever nourished because of you. Thank you!

To all my friends, family, clients, and those who brighten my world and lift me up, and who keep me laughing, loving, and embracing life . . . THANK YOU.

To you. I see you. I love you. Keep going.

ABOUT THE AUTHOR AND SPEAKER

Krista Ryan is a Professional Certified Coach (PCC), facilitator, trainer, and professional speaker. As a highly sought after business coach and workplace performance expert, Krista's focus is on Leadership Excellence and Workplace Success. She supports industries around the globe, from small family-owned businesses to Fortune 100 companies, by helping effectively navigate wild success or uncertainty and change while promoting collaboration, communication, and confidence.

With nearly two decades of experience as a human resources director, Krista is the CEO and founder of KFG Coaching, LLC. She's a Bravely Pro Coach, a global coaching organization, and a Room Tilter with Limitless Minds, a mental conditioning organization that unites personal growth with business success through the power of neutral thinking.

Krista is also a motivational speaker through the National Speakers Association. Through her creative and engaging style of speaking and coaching, she works both at the corporate level and individually. She has helped thousands of people take the steps to KFG.

When Krista is not on stage or supporting her clients through workshops and coaching, she can be found spending time with her husband and 3 children, relaxing in her home state of Minnesota or traveling the globe in search of the world's best oyster bar!

To learn more, and to connect directly with Krista Ryan, go to KristaRyan.com.